© 2026 Cora Ellen Oleson. All rights reserved.

No part of this publication may be reproduced, distributed, or transmitted in any form or by any means, including photocopying, recording, or other electronic or mechanical methods, without the prior written permission of the publisher, except as permitted by U.S. copyright law.

ISBN: 979-8-218-91531-5 (paperback)
ISBN: 979-8-218-92705-5 (ebook)

Library of Congress Control Number: 2026902456

For privacy reasons, names, locations, and dates may have been changed.

A healing journey dedicated to my children.

"You are the source of my joy,
the center of my world,
and the whole of my heart".

- Richard Smallwood

Prologue

"**She has blonde** hair, to my brown, vibrant blue eyes, and an easy smile. Not the oldest with responsibilities like me. She has older and younger siblings to play with. I am the oldest child, the oldest grandchild on both sides of my family, raised on reminders to set the right example. While my younger siblings and cousins get to play, I am often asked to stay and help. Mom lays out my clothes, carefully brushes my hair, ties it with bows. I am neat and contained. But she is free and wild.

I don't remember how we met, only that we were inseparable from then on. She is my opposite in many ways, but we are so similar. Every day I would ask Mom when we could play. We weren't in the same class but would walk to school together and waited for each other during recess. We ran into each other's arms every time like it had been too long. With her, I am not the oldest, I am not the example, I am simply me.

I cried when Mom said we were moving. I was told to say goodbye, and it felt so final. Learning that some losses don't come with closure—only distance, memory, and the quiet ache of a lost friendship. A friendship that felt just as important as family. I wondered if I'd ever see her again. Years later, I would see that moment as the first real friendship and the time it left."

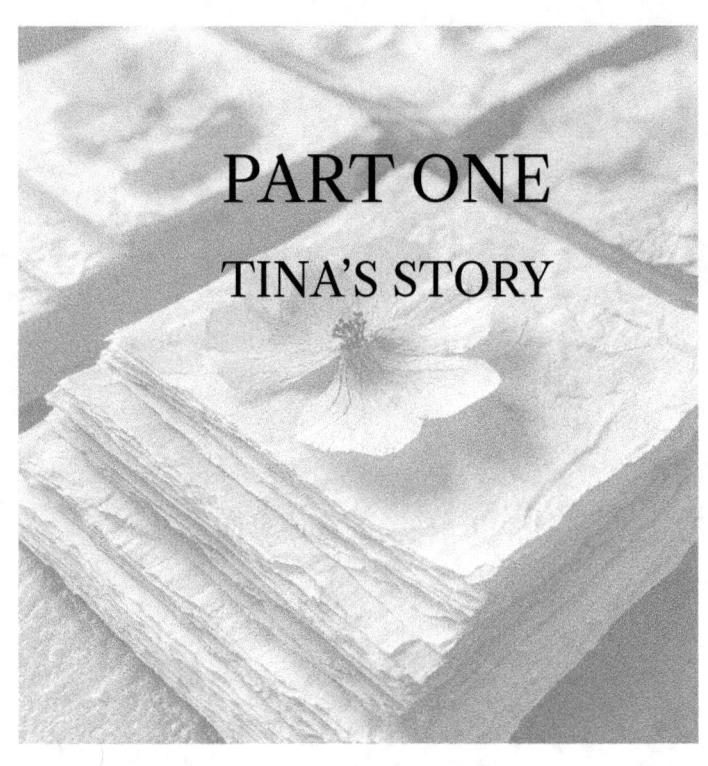

PART ONE
TINA'S STORY

"The only way out is through"
\- Robert Frost

ONE

I remember how soft her hands were when we would run through the field together and watched how she was tucked in bed by her mom and then her dad at night when I slept over. I felt how loved, special, and wanted she was. The way her parents lit up when she entered a room and wondered how it was decided that she was chosen to be born into a home like this. I love my family, but I didn't get hugged and held like that. At least not now where there were so many kids, and home often felt chaotic. I was only five years old, but this was the first time I wondered about life.

She lived around the corner from me. We went to the same school and church. People joked that where Tina was, Tara wasn't far behind. It felt true, like we were connected by something unseen. We even had matching small birthmarks on the back of our left arms. Well, maybe they were just moles, but we both had them, and it felt special. Proof that we belonged to each other somehow.

Only a few years later, both our families moved away. No big goodbye or understanding of what was being lost. Just distance, introduced before we knew how to name it. Still, something of her stayed with me.

A big family always means you have someone to play with and opportunities to fight. For the most part, we all played together, riding bikes, skateboards, and playing baseball in the backyard. I am number four of six and often felt overwhelmed finding places to hide just to be alone. My favorite three were inside the huge raspberry bushes, lying on my back in the tall grass watching the clouds drifting across the sky, and perched on the side-yard fence or on the roof during lightning storms. Although I'm the one hiding, I knew that no one was ever looking for me.

Mom grew beautiful vegetable gardens and made the most delicious raisin bread and cinnamon rolls. I remember how much attention I got and love I felt from her when I would help in the garden and clean up the kitchen after she baked. Going downstairs to be at eye level with the kitchen floor to see what spots I missed. Mom really liked that I did this. I know because I heard her telling people. I found ways to follow her and do things to make her proud of me. Everyone called me her little helper. So I did more. It was warm in her light.

As the years went on, I stayed close in her shadow. It was nowhere near Dad. Fights and arguments that spread to include my older brothers grew as the years passed. I found a hill at the end of our neighborhood to stay on for hours sometimes. Just long enough for things to quiet down. I prayed a lot, asking God if he was there. I spent a lot of time looking up. It was magical and mysterious.

I shared a room with my older sister Claire who really wanted nothing to do with me. I tried to be like her and follow her which just made her mad. It didn't take too long for me to learn to stay away but it's hard when your beds are only feet apart. She would do and say things that made me cry and then she would laugh calling me a baby. When her friends would come around, they made it a game to run away and lock the bedroom door so I couldn't get in.

In the middle of the 7th grade, Mom left. She went back home to California with Grandma. We were told that the two oldest would move out (Ben and Byron), the youngest two (Mark and Olivia) would go to California at the end of the school year, and the middle two could choose (me and Claire).

I hated that Mom left. I mean, I hated that Mom left me. Home was a place I escaped from often to my hill. The fights between Dad and my brothers echoed through the neighborhood. I would leave for hours and watch to see if anyone would look for me. No one ever did. Food was scarce. It always had been, but now worse with Mom gone. Dad just didn't seem to care, and begging for a ride to school happened every morning. He would often sign a late slip and had us walk even through the cold and snow. I was always in charge of Mark and Olivia.

I defended Mom a lot for leaving. I don't know why because I was confused and had no answers, but it really upset me to hear unkind things said about her. Dad and I lived in the same house, but he didn't have much to do with me and often made comments that weren't nice to and about Byron and me specifically.

Both Ben and Byron moved out. I don't know where they went, but I heard Byron was emancipated. He was only sixteen. Although home was hard, school became the place I preferred to be. I usually got lunch and sometimes breakfast if I could make it in time.

I had so many best friends, none of whom knew about my home life. I was just fun to them, and I loved the escape. When they found out I would be moving away, they threw a big party at the end of the year to say goodbye. I was sad and scared. I hadn't seen or heard from Mom in all these months and had never been to California. Grandma had only come to see us once since I was born, so I didn't have many memories of her.

***

It's like I was dropped off in a new world! Palm trees, the smell of the ocean and a fresh start. It was summer now, and with Mom working, the four of us kids were scooped up into a group of families from church that would do things together like beach days, parks, crafts, picnics, and parties.

We were around family I had never heard of before. Great Aunts and Uncles, second, third and fourth cousins. We joined Grandma every other Sunday to bring groceries and spend the day with Great Grandma up north on her farm. It sat on many acres of land, but the home was so small. To get to the front door, we had to walk through the gated front yard, and the chickens would chase me, pecking at my legs. She shared stories of growing up here with no indoor plumbing, and there were many things we would repair on our visits. We would race across the field trying to avoid all the cow-pies. I had never been this close to cows just grazing in the fields. I loved coming here.

Soon school started and I was fascinated that you walked outdoors to get to your classes, and the cafeteria was outside since the weather was so nice. I would eat my lunch under one of the many palm trees. I made a lot of friends, had babysitting jobs, and money to spend. We also had a swimming pool in our townhouse complex, and I was on a volleyball team. Life was really wonderful!

Mom worked, so I would take care of the house. After school, I would find a list of groceries she would leave for me and cash for that night's dinner. I would walk to the grocery store, do laundry, set the table, make dinner, and help the kids with their homework. For the most part, Claire, Mark, and Olivia were out playing with their friends. I loved helping Mom, and she really appreciated me. I felt needed, important, and loved here.

Mom started dating. I would babysit the kids when she would go out. When she returned from a date, she would wake me up to tell me about him. She was more than a mom to me; she was my best friend. She was so happy, and I liked our new life.

Sometimes Dad would call, and by the end, we were in tears, feeling sorry for our happiness and his loneliness. Mark was starting to fight with us more often and had moments where he got really angry and would lash out. It never lasted long, and he was a funny, happy boy again.

Mom started dating a new guy who was coming around pretty regularly. Not long after he was in the picture, my sisters and I were told that Mark went back to live with Dad. I don't remember saying goodbye or even knowing he would be leaving. There were no more calls with Dad, and it was like Mark just disappeared.

The more Bill came around, the more things changed. He lived over an hour away and wanted Mom to come to him, but she struggled to stay awake at night to drive home. They decided that I should go with her to keep her company on the drive. Bill also had a son my age, so they wanted the two of us to hang out during their date—somewhere else. This son was not someone I wanted to be around. One time we were in the pool, and he kept dunking me and holding my head down. I was flailing and hitting him, gulping so much water trying to tell him to stop. He was a bully and mean, but I didn't tell Mom.

Not long after they met, Mom shared that they were getting married. They left for a weekend, and it was done. With us three girls and his son still in school, they planned to live separately and move in together that summer. So I continued to drive with Mom to see him. I noted that she almost always went to him. They found a beautiful home in a really nice neighborhood. I was saying goodbye again to my many new, amazing friends. It was hard to keep moving, but Mom said this was the last time.

Now we were living with Bill and his son. Like the last move, we immediately were swept into a huge group through church. The youth were the focus here, and I got to waterski, sail, go to house parties, beach parties that included youth from the entire Bay Area, beach volleyball, football games, professional sporting events, beach bonfires, camping—endless opportunities and friends. I couldn't believe how wonderful everyone was.

One babysitting job I had was to travel to Santa Barbara with a family so I could watch the kids during certain parts of a long weekend wedding they were attending. They picked me up after school in a massive palace on wheels to drive down the coast, staying on the beach and eating out at fancy restaurants. I had a Belgian waffle covered in fruit and whipping cream every morning, and they were so amused that I had never seen one before. They even gave me extra shopping money and a day in the town to buy some new clothes and sunglasses.

Home was interesting. It felt like all Bill was doing was trying to separate me from my mom. I wanted to go to the grocery store with her and cook with her, but he pulled me aside to let me know that I was not going to do that anymore. They ate separately from us three girls; his son got to eat in his room. He was very strict with us, but his son could do all the things we were told not to do. Bill said it was because we were raised differently.

When I would go out with friends, they would tell me that Bill was following us. I started running just to get permission to leave the house. He needed to know where I was and who I was with at all times. He followed Claire also, who just started driving. His son and I ended up having a few classes together at the new school. He was terrible to me and harassing with his friends. I tried to tell my mom, but she would tell Bill, and I would get in trouble and not be able to go out with friends.

My regular chores included cleaning up the dishes from his son's room. Even if he was sleeping, I was told to knock and then quietly gather his dishes. We were never allowed to have food in our rooms, but we couldn't question the unfairness. His son loved telling everyone at school that I was his maid. I hated them both.

Claire and I were the only kids to share a room. She has never been too kind to me and resented that all of her friends were also my friends. She didn't like it when people referred to us as 'the girls' and tried to keep me excluded from things. Sometimes she would say something to Bill, and I was restricted to my room for a reason not told to me, missing out on some fun event. I was in trouble with him a lot, and it was clear I was the only one.

TWO

One day, Mom came home from work early and told us that Bill's son was in the hospital. We weren't told why, but Bill hung a few photos he took in the hallway of them smiling on the hospital bed. I learned later that he got so drunk he had alcohol poisoning. I said something under my breath and paid for that.

While he was still in the hospital, my sisters were gone and Mom was at work. Bill came home early, sneaking quietly in the house to my room, and told me to sit down. He clearly planned this. I was on the edge of my bed, and he screamed at me about how I better never drink alcohol and what he would do to me if I did. I was scared. I was mad, and I really, really hated this man. As soon as Mom came home, I'm going to tell her!

Planning what I would say and watching for when Mom was alone. I saw her walk into her bedroom and knew Bill was still in the kitchen, so I ran down the hall to her room and shut the door behind me. I started talking fast, and Mom just stared at me. Bill then threw the door open, and he and I started fighting. I looked at my mom and said, "Aren't you going to do something?" I remember her saying that she spent nineteen years being a mom to us kids and given all she had, and it is her turn now. Then she asked why I didn't want her to be happy. She turned and left the room so she didn't have to hear anymore. He let me have it. I was restricted to the house with extra chores for an unspecified time.

Claire refused to talk to me and pretended I wasn't there. We shared the same room, so this was ridiculous and would look at herself in the mirror talking (to herself) about where she was going and how much fun she would have. Bill told me that I was upsetting my mother, so it would be best if I ate once everyone was done.

Within days, I was being driven to the airport. I didn't understand what was happening. I was bawling, looking at my mom, and asking why she was doing this. She just looked away. Bill was happy though, and so was Claire.

I cried the whole flight home, and my eyes were puffy, red, and stung. People looked, but no one talked to me on the plane or as I tried to navigate a connection in Vegas. This was the first time I had flown. Everything I had with me fit in my school bag, and I didn't know what was in there.

When I came off the plane back in Colorado, there was Mark!! We never saw or spoke with him after he was sent away. I ran and hugged him so tightly. He wriggled out of my arms, embarrassed. Dad seemed really happy to see me too. They drove in a little red MGB convertible with a huge stuffed bear for me that could only fit because the top was down. He said it was mine when I turned 16, and that was exciting. The ride home was full of questions about my sisters and Bill, mostly. Dad didn't hesitate to tell us both that Mom got rid of us and had plenty to say about Bill.

It was weird to be back in the house. When I left, there were seven of us there and a house full of furniture. Now we were three and a couple of mismatched chairs as the furniture all went to Mom. Mark said they spent the whole morning cleaning, but it didn't look like it. They had my old room ready for me with a sleeping bag on the floor and a promise to work on getting a mattress.

It didn't take long to learn that Dad wanted me there to take care of the cleaning, cooking, and whatever else he and Mark needed. My system was shocked into a new reality again. Dad was either thrusting more work on me or he was just gone. I was fourteen, and Mark was twelve.

There was no food in the house anywhere. Sometimes Dad would wake us in the middle of the night with some chicken he brought home from the store, and we would devour it. No plates or forks. Just hungry and pulling the meat off the bones.

Old habits die hard, and when it got to be too much, I would leave the house. It was too cold for the hill, so I would lie down on the floor of the back seat in the car. Somewhere he couldn't find me to give me more work to do where I could just be alone. Under the driver seat, I saw a McDonald's wrapper. Fury took over, and I went in screaming at him that Mark hadn't eaten and how selfish he was. He told me that I had a bad attitude and a chip on my shoulder.

It was the middle of a school year, but I was back with my old friends and became pretty popular as the tanned blonde from California. No one knew about my home life or why I was being bounced around. It was kind of like before I left. When rumors would get around the school, neighborhood, and church about my situation, I was the girl no good family wanted their kids around. Little did they know that their kids were doing things they had to explain to me.

No more babysitting jobs to earn some money now either. Once the word spread that I was a bad kid from a bad home, I usually got to see the darker side of people. Oh, and the amount of girl-enemies from groups I didn't even know with their dirty looks and mean comments at school only took hours into my first day to appear. At first, I wondered what I had done, and it felt really bad, but when I realized they were just being mean, I met them there and was happy when I had a clever comeback that would embarrass them.

Summer break came, and Dad said we were leaving as he was on sabbatical at another university for the summer. I had made plans to hang out with my friends and didn't even get the chance to tell them I was leaving the state. It wasn't too bad though. We stayed in student housing and got to hit the university cafeteria every day, bowl, play video games there, and had access to the community pool. Mark and I walked everywhere and spent the whole summer together.

When we returned to Colorado, Dad talked about moving into an apartment and how Mark and I would share a room. I told him that we were too old to share a room, and he should share with Mark or get enough rooms for us all. He did not like my attitude, and we fought hard. Our fights got physical. He would push or drag me. I would run away once I got a good hit in.

***

I spent time back on that hill, but fear set in, so I would walk to keep moving. I was angry. Angry at Dad. Angry at Mom. Angry at Bill. I felt scared and mad and unwanted and unloved. I even yelled to the sky for God to help me. At the beginning, I would leave for hours and then quietly return and avoid Dad. We would go on like this until another fight ensued. Sometimes I knew I came back too soon and would have to leave again. I got better about bringing a coat as it was cold outside, especially at night. Mark just hid somewhere in the house or around a corner. Dad took his rage out on me, so I felt like I was protecting Mark.

Dad's a professor, so there would be times he would not be working, and he would travel to singles events in other states for days or weeks at a time. I came home to see the washer and dryer were gone, and another time the stereo was missing. I knew he sold them to pay for his trips and dates. I was so angry and disgusted with him.

He would have a friend from church drive him to the airport so his car would be in the driveway. Not that I knew he was leaving or when he would come back. I decided I would use it to get us to school. Mark and I would scour his dresser and clothes to find any change we could to buy gas. I had missed so much school at this point and remember feeling stupid and so far behind.

I dropped Mark off at the elementary school and then drove myself to the Jr. High. The teachers would call on me since I had missed so much class, and I got humiliated. I stopped going to those classes and would hang around the hallways or bathrooms. Until I got sent to the principal's office, where I learned someone told on me for driving a car. I tried parking across the street, but they were watching me now.

So I did the only thing I knew to do and stopped going. No one from the school ever reached out or seemed to care or notice. I didn't know how to feed Mark and couldn't wash clothes, so I decided to drop him off at a family's house from church where his best friend lived. I didn't talk to them but just left him there, hoping they would just let him stay over for a while. They did.

Eventually, Mark would return, but we did this often. I would visit some of my new friends and they told their parents I was sixteen to explain the driving thing. I would get to wash my clothes there and got some from girl friends. I started dating a boy, and he would bring me things from home for Mark and me: clothes, food, tampons, and toilet paper. I was embarrassed but so appreciative.

Mark and I would go to the grocery store, and I would carefully spend the dollar or two we had on food and swing by the bakery and deli a handful of times to grab samples. Sometimes the workers would remove the sample container seeing that we had already come by. Little did I know at the time that Mark started stealing while we were there.

Once a box was left on our doorstep filled with milk, eggs, cereal, apples, oranges, rice, oats, and chocolate. We never knew who left it there and definitely didn't tell Dad when he returned. I think it was a young family from church that I would see drive by sometimes. They didn't live anywhere close to us, but I saw their car parked a few houses away a time or two.

Well, our bishop caught wind of Dad leaving us and called the house, saying he needed to speak with me. I remember him asking where my dad was, and I said he was home or working; it changed through the interrogation. He knew he was gone because a church member was dropping him off and then picking him up from the airport a couple of weeks later. He said that if my Dad was leaving us, he would have to call child protection services, so I did everything to lie and seem calm. I don't know where my information came from but believed Mark and I would be separated and sent away. I would run away with him before I let that happen.

This time when Dad returned, he was picked up by the bishop at the airport. I found out because he came in like a train at me for telling on him. Slaps and shoves were flying, and I really got in his face this time.

He grabbed me by the nape of my neck with a handful of hair and shoved me into a chair, holding me down while he played a Phil Donahue clip about women and PMS. I got so angry and yelled that any woman who disagrees with him magically has PMS while I bolted up out of the chair, turned, swung as hard as I could with my fist to his face, and ran out the door. I had no idea what PMS was.

This time I didn't grab a coat, and it was winter. Rage has a way of heating you from the inside, but eventually, the night and cold pierced through my skin like needles. The wind bit my face but froze any tears before they could fall. I walked for so many hours well into the dark of the night.

There was a group of people laughing and headed to a car nearby. A few guys started yelling "hey babe," so I kept my head down and walked even faster, trying to avoid them. One guy ran over to me though and really looked concerned, telling me to stop. He said they were headed to a house party and I could come with them to get warm. I looked over at the car and the group that was waiting for him and said yes.

I was scared but was a lot more cold. I don't know how the door shut with so many of us piled on top of each other. We got to this house, and there were people everywhere! All college-aged but probably not college-bound. When people started asking who I was, this group of probably ten who I came with said I was with them and to leave me alone. I was warm and there was food.

The parties raged and faded as the night turned to day. The things I was offered and saw there educated a pretty sheltered girl quickly, but I knew I wanted only to stay warm. The guys asked if I had been drinking and said that I don't drink, so from that time on, I became a designated driver. I dropped people off and picked people up in someone's car one party to the next. We did this day after day. I remember waking up in a small apartment once where bodies were sleeping (or passed out) everywhere, including the kitchen counters. Girls would give me clothes, and everyone seemed to have cold pizza.

THREE

I would go back home for a while until the next fight. Once, when I returned home, having been gone almost two weeks, Dad wanted to talk to me. He said that I would be driving him to the airport and picking him up now. That I was not to drive the car outside of that and made me promise. Plus the tank was always on empty anyway.

Now I knew when he would be leaving and returning and told him we needed gas and food money, or I wouldn't do it. He gave me a credit card that he said only had enough on it for the gas to and from the airport and agreed to buy some groceries. This worked pretty well in my opinion. I still spent time with my new friends as the families of my school and church friends wouldn't let them see me. I never drank, smoked, or took any substances, and no one ever took advantage of me with the wall of protectors that saved me that cold night. Dad often talked of emancipating me. It wasn't a threat. He had done this to Byron, so I knew he meant it. I was fifteen now, and I knew I'd have a hard time getting a job with no home or transportation.

Many months went by like this until the phone rang and would turn my world upside down again that Sunday in January. The phone rang, and I picked up in the kitchen at the same time Dad picked up in his bedroom. It was a lady from church, and I heard my name, so I didn't hang up. She told my Dad that a young girl needed a family influence, and her sister would take me. Dad only asked if they wanted any money, and the answer was no. She started to offer more information, but Dad already agreed. Before I knew what was happening, I was on a one-way flight out of state. Again.

I was so mad and kept wracking my brain for how and when to run. I fought with him and kept saying I didn't want to go. It was literally within twenty-four hours that I was on that plane. I didn't know who they were, and they didn't know who I was, so I dreamed that I would just walk past them and keep going.

I don't remember crying anymore. I felt numb and so unwanted. I hadn't come up with any plan, and it was winter, so I couldn't just sleep at a park. I couldn't imagine how I would go from having no supervision to living with strangers. When I got off the plane, there was this young family holding a sign with my name on it. They had a little girl who was about three years old. I just walked over to them, touched their sign, and flatly said, "That's me".

I could tell I was making them uncomfortable, as they surely believed they were doing a good deed, so I faked a smile and made sure I was friendly. I knew that as soon as I could figure out a plan, I would just leave.

They seemed nice enough, but when we got to their house, they didn't have a room for me. I was to sleep on the couch or with the little girl. I really didn't like this and desperately wanted to be alone. When they showed me the rest of the house and the unfinished basement, I asked if I could stay down there. I told the man, Jack, that I had helped build homes and I could help build a room down there. He was open to the idea and pulled out some camping equipment, allowing me to sleep there.

The next day, I was taken to church with them. Everyone was asking all the questions I didn't want to answer and didn't really know how to answer. Some boys were too friendly, and some girls watched. I remember this routine, so I tried to brush the guys away, even though they were some of the only friendly ones in my classes. Word spread quickly about the new girl without a family.

Again, it was the middle of the school year. Trying to navigate the most massive school I'd ever been in with a schedule that took me to several different floors into classes I hadn't been in for such a long time was terrifying, but I wouldn't let anyone see that. All I could think about was running.

A few girls from church saw me there and came over to my locker to help me find my next class and invite me to meet them for lunch. I was so relieved and grateful. While they were at my locker looking at my class schedule, a group of boys that seemed to know them also came over and were really friendly.

One guy stayed behind when the bell rang and offered to walk me to my next class. He was sweet, and I couldn't stop smiling at his attention. He would always find me and even sat with the large group of girls to have lunch with us. His friends were always teasing something to the effect of him liking me. And I liked that. I learned that he was pretty popular at the school. Some girls would warn me about him, but it didn't make any sense for who I saw him to be.

I was hyper-focused on finding my classes before the bell rang to not draw attention. Teachers wanted me to stand up and introduce myself and tell them where I had come from. I hated this so much and tried to say as little as possible. I think teachers can be so clueless. Never in the now three states of different schools did a teacher ever reach out to see if I was okay.

Every time the bell rang, Jace was waiting for me. There were others that were really friendly and offered to show me around and get me to my next class, but when they saw Jace, they backed off. I was so happy to see a friendly face and really liked him. He claimed me pretty fast, and not long after, I was being introduced as his girl.

Jace was not just at my school, but he also went to the same church, and his family knew of Jack and Emma and my living arrangement with them. I really clung to him and other girlfriends I had met. They were my family now.

Jace told me he loved me, and when we graduated, we were going to get married and move to Montana. He would pick me up in his truck if he needed to run an errand for his mom and said he didn't just want to be away from me. I was in love!

***

I spent many nights and weekends working with Jack to frame and drywall my own room that was now taking shape. I even got a bathroom! My jaw started to hurt, but I didn't want to complain, so I just kept it to myself. Until I couldn't. The pain became excruciating. I stopped eating and eventually let Jack and Emma know. They looked inside my mouth just to find that all of my wisdom teeth were piercing through my gums.

They were a kind family who volunteered to take in a girl, but they weren't legal guardians and had no insurance for me. This wasn't a registered foster home either, so I didn't qualify for state insurance. I was told that they reached out to my dad to see if there was any dental insurance, but he told them no and that he didn't have any money.

Jack and Emma didn't have the money to cover this either - especially without the insurance offset. I don't know how they did it, but with their church connections, they found a young guy in dental school who was going to try and help. He didn't have a license yet but obtained a little Novocaine, gauze, and some pliers. We met on a weekend and were not in a dental office but outside the mall.

I did everything to hold as still as possible as the last of the Novocaine was gone, and it didn't numb my gums. The pain was severe, but this was my only chance. All my teeth came out in broken pieces. My jaw hurt so badly, and my gums were swollen and so sore I thought I'd never be able to eat again.

The pain was overwhelming. I remember the look on this guy's face. He had no idea what he had gotten himself into, and I could see his fear. The back of my head had a lump from where it was pressed down while pulling in the other direction.

By the grace of God, he finished. I didn't eat for days, and Jack and Emma were told to keep checking for infection. I don't know how he did it, but he got them all out with no complications. The recovery was long, and the bruises on my jaw took even longer to go away. I asked a couple of times to see if my dad checked back, but he never did. I felt so disgusted, and I couldn't believe he would do this to his own child. I thanked Jack and Emma frequently for taking me in.

Between school, sports, and friends, I was only at their house when I had to be. When school ended, I got a job at the downtown frozen yogurt shop and was making money and driving a lot more now that I could pay for my gas. I loved this new freedom and still spent all my time with either Jace or my girlfriends. Now almost seventeen, I was excited to dream of being roommates with my best friend once we graduated and planning a life with Jace.

At the end of July, one of Jace's best friends reached out to shake my hand after a baseball game they played in. I thought he was joking around, so I shook it and felt a note. He looked at me with eyes that told me not to say anything. I put it in my pocket, and that night, found it forgetting it was there. In it, he writes that Jace is seeing other girls, and he thinks I'm nice and don't deserve to be lied to. I felt angry at him and thought he was just trying to break us up.

Next time I saw him, he said the same thing, and I told him I didn't believe him. He then reminded me of a campout he and a bunch of friends were going to that I initially was invited to, but Jace told me it was just going to be the guys this time. His friend told me that is a lie and there are many girls going. I told him I trust Jace and didn't believe him, he just told me that I could go and see for myself.

The nagging of my thoughts wouldn't let me sleep. I didn't tell anyone but decided to drive up there anyway. It was four days away, and everything was really great between Jace and me. I was sure his friend was lying. But I drove up the canyon anyway after dark. There was a large group of about forty people around a bonfire. They were drinking, so I figured that is why he didn't want me there. I stayed to see if I could find him in the crowd. It took a while for my eyes to adjust, and I did find him. With his hands up the skirt of a girl from school I thought was my friend.

It was a windy dirt road to get out of there. I was devastated and sobbing uncontrollably. When he called the next day to see me, I waited to see if he would come clean, but he acted normal. I asked about the campout, and he lied, telling me it was just a couple of guys hanging out. I yelled at him that I went up there and saw him, and he quickly blamed the alcohol for what he did. His friend was right. I told him I never wanted to see him again and hung up.

I cried for days and days. When I wouldn't take his calls or come to the door, he would drop off flowers with a note that everyone is lying and that I'm the only one. My girlfriends told me he was seen with her every day. He was still lying to me, and I was such a fool. As much as I tried to hide, I saw him too with many different girls.

In no time, he acted like he didn't know me. He started spreading a lot of lies and saying horrible things about me. I felt shattered.

FOUR

It was the end of summer, the last weekend before school started, when my dad called. He was in the state on his way to drop Claire back in California after she had been in Colorado to visit friends. He had another singles event an hour from me and asked if I would pick Claire and Mark up for the weekend. Jack and Emma were happy to meet some of my family and welcomed them.

I called into work and drove down to pick them up. We went shopping and to the movies before heading back to the house that evening. Claire would criticize my hair and clothes and brag about her 'Cali life'. I tried to show off how happy I was and how great things were going for me. The next day, we went to church, and then it was time to take them back to where my dad had been staying.

Claire had bought the new Scorpions tape the night before, quickly called "shotgun" and pushed it into the cassette player of the car. Mark had tried to race to the front seat, but she beat him, and he reluctantly climbed in the back. As we were pulling out of the driveway, Emma came out waving us down, telling us to stop. She had somewhere to go and needed to switch cars. This happened often as she had a bad back and couldn't drive their truck as it was a manual, and the clutch was hard to push in.

We switched over to the truck, and Mark was happy because it only had a bench seat, so we all rode up front. Claire was not happy though, as this old truck didn't have a radio or any way for her to play the tape. We were already running late, but she wouldn't let it go.

I ran back in the house to grab my boombox but didn't have batteries for it. Jack helped us get it working, and Claire was finally happy. Mark was goofing off, sticking his hand in parts of the truck bed that were rusted through to the other side. We were loading in with Claire in the middle. The boombox reached from part of my leg across both of hers and onto Mark's. It was big!

We couldn't find any seatbelts except for the passenger seat where Mark was. Emma leaned in the window next to Mark and asked when I'd be back and to drive safely as the tires aren't great. I agreed, and we pulled away.

This truck is so old that every time I needed to shift gears, Claire would have to move the boombox as the long shaft was in the steering column. The clutch was so tight that I had to stand to get it all the way in. We laughed about this and how even with the windows all the way up, the wind coming through them was loud enough that we had to scream on the freeway to hear each other. Claire had the music blasting, and we were on our way.

There were a series of highway connections that were to take us to Dad, but after some time on the road, I didn't recognize the busy highway we should have been on. We were heading west and must have missed the last connection to head south. This freeway was empty as we were now out of the city.

I looked over my shoulder to get into the far right lane and saw that we just missed an exit. As we went under the small overpass, I noticed raindrops falling on the windshield. I yelled for Claire to turn off the music so they could help me find a place to turn around.

Just as the music stopped, I felt the truck drop, and loud scraping was heard and felt under the front driver's side. I was scared and quickly tried to stop the truck by standing on the clutch and slamming the brakes.

We were not slowing down, and both the steering and brakes were now locked. I could not move the steering wheel and couldn't shift or brake. This highway had three large lanes going west with a large median ditch between the east and westbound lanes. It curved back and forth for miles. We were the only car in sight.

I'm screaming to tell Mark and Claire that I can't control the truck while I'm pulling on the wheel as hard as I can. "I think we lost a tire!" I reached down to see if I could turn the key when the back passenger side dropped with more scraping. I hoped that the rims on the road would slow us down, but the road was starting to curve to the right, and we moved from the slow lane into the fast lane, and the mile markers were folding under the hood as we hit them.

We were heading for the median, and there was nothing I could do. Claire was screaming at me, and Mark was crying. Then the front passenger side dropped, and I realized we were riding on one tire only. I yelled out "SHIT" and immediately thought that we were about to die, and I just cussed.

The truck was tipping over on the driver's side. I felt the passenger side lifting off the road. The weight of Mark and Claire was pushing me against the door. The door flew open, exposing the median grasses whizzing beside me. I'm gripping the steering wheel as tight as I can, and my knees are pressing hard against the dashboard to try and stay inside the cab.

We were moving at such a fast speed. I'm pushing as hard as I can against the weight of them on me as I'm falling out. I'm losing my grip but holding on as tight as I can. Thoughts of waterskiing instructions came to my mind in a flash as you are told that once you fall down, you are supposed to let go of the rope or you will be dragged. I was trying to decide when to let go.

We are sliding on the driver's side, speeding across the median. We have moved down the median and now up the other side, and just as we reach the oncoming lanes, I am out the door holding the steering wheel with one hand only, being dragged on the road alongside the truck. The road curves again, and the truck is now turning back into the median, back onto its feet, lifting me up. I let go and try quickly to get up when my arm brushes the spinning back tire, tearing at my arm, and I drop low.

Laying on the road, I am watching through the open door as the truck falls back into the median and rolls, ejecting Claire out the driver-side door, and continues to go up the far side of the median. Flipping again back onto the westbound lanes on its feet, finally stopping on the far shoulder. I don't see Mark anywhere.

I am in the fast lane of the eastbound lanes, facing the median. My leg from above the knee to my foot is shredded, and like a hose, a vein in my ankle is extended out and spraying blood. I sit up, reaching down, and grab it tight.

I am scanning the entirety of the crumpled journey, searching for Mark. Claire is below me a ways down in the bottom of the median, climbing up on all fours in my direction, screaming that she is going to kill me for killing her brother. I didn't want to live if he died anyway. She climbs up a little ways and then falls and rolls down, repeating this over and over. I prop myself up on the hand not holding the firehose vein and look behind me to see a car come into view.

A car stops in the middle of the road that was coming eastbound toward me, leaving the doors of their car open and running over. The man takes off his shirt and wraps it tightly around my knee. I feel no pain, just terror that Mark is dead.

The woman introduces them, saying that they are a doctor and a nurse, and start asking me questions. I tell them my name but don't care about the other things they are wanting. I need them to find Mark. I keep telling them to find Mark, and they keep repeating that there is a girl in the median and they are going to help her too. I keep telling them to find Mark, and they must just think I'm in shock, confusing my sister with my brother.

They ask me where I live, and I tell them. They are asking for my parents' names and how to reach them. I tried to explain that this is my brother and sister, and I live in a foster home. Claire lives in California with my mom, and Mark lives in Colorado with my dad, but my dad is at a conference. They keep asking questions, trying to understand what I am telling them.

The pain is starting to expose itself to me. There was so much blood that it had soaked through his shirt and covered the road around me. Other people had now joined the scene. Someone was carrying up the sweatshirt from near Claire to offer as a wrap for my leg when she started screaming not to get blood on it. I begged them to give her back her sweatshirt. She bragged the previous day about this white sweatshirt she kept from one of her old boyfriends. I didn't want it.

The distance from me to the truck was so far on this massive highway that I couldn't see into it. I strained my eyes, hoping to make out his head and any movement, but I just couldn't make out anything. I was repeating over and over that Mark was still in the truck, but they were busy with Claire and managing the mass amount of blood under my leg. I was crying out to God to take me and not Mark.

The people gathering had now grown into many different groups and were talking to each other, deciding who would drive to get help. I heard them repeat that the ambulance was taking too long and they should just transport us themselves. Finally, sirens could be heard, and the man said it took them over forty minutes. I was so relieved as the pain was more than I could bear.

There was a semi that stopped near the truck, and I heard a conversation that the driver found a boy in the truck with a head injury, and he was non-responsive. They said he would take the ambulance alone. I was crying and begging God to save him.

I watched as his ambulance was loaded with a stretcher and sped away. Several police cars had now arrived. Some were going to the semi driver, some to Claire, and two to me.

FIVE

The police said they were able to speak with Jack and understood now and the things I was telling them. For the tenth time, I was asked to tell them what had happened. I watched as a few police were out measuring and taking pictures of the road, truck, me, and tire pieces. They placed a couple of tire pieces in baggies. When they got closer, I heard them say that the blood from my leg started seventy-five feet from where I lay. This is how far they determined I was dragged. No one was talking to me anymore, just about me.

Finally, a second ambulance came. I could see that they wrapped a blanket around Claire's shoulders and were walking her to the ambulance. She was hysterical.

I was fitted with a huge neck brace and lifted onto a stretcher into the ambulance also. Claire was inconsolable and screaming. She wanted her Scorpions tape and her sweatshirt and wouldn't stop, so someone said they were going to get it so she would calm down. I asked to get the neck brace off as it felt like it was pulling my head off my shoulders and hurt, but they wouldn't.

I couldn't move my head to see Claire next to me but could hear her yelling at me. I asked for Tylenol for the pain but was told I couldn't have anything. They pierced my arm with the largest needle I have ever seen.

The ambulance bed felt like I was lying on cement, and every bump bounced me hard. We got to a small hospital, and I kept asking about Mark. They placed me in a space only big enough for this stretcher with curtains pulled all around. They continued to ask the same things again. I told them I wouldn't answer any more questions until they told me where Mark was.

A nurse was called over, and she brushed some hair out of my face and told me that Mark is okay!!! That I am hurt far worse than either of them. I am so relieved and thank God. She said we are all at the same hospital, but they cannot help me here, and I need to be transported to the city. She tries to prepare me for the possibility of losing my leg, but I don't care and only beg for them to let me see Mark and Claire before I go.

They cleaned out my left arm where the tire spun into it with what felt like fire. Wrapping that and my right wrist that was broken. I couldn't get anything for the pain or water for my thirst, but I didn't care anymore since I knew Mark and Claire would be okay. I was alert, felt everything, and wished I would just pass out. I only cried when I thought Mark died and again when I knew they were both going to be okay.

There was a conversation outside of my little sheeted room about a helicopter, but there was no insurance or legal guardian to sign for it, so they would have to wait for the ambulance. Waiting for another hour before it arrived. A doctor I had met before pulled a little of the curtain back and said he had a group of interns with him. He asked if I would be okay if they took a look at my leg. I said that I wasn't going anywhere, so sure. As the doctor started lifting my bandages, he was talking to the interns about the road rash with a gaping opening from above my knee to my toes and not sure of the damage underneath. Two of the interns passed out. They quickly ushered everyone out, and I was alone again.

The ambulance arrived, and on my way, I got to see Claire, who told me that she had scratches on her back and had convulsed a couple of times, so they will keep her overnight. She was smiling and said she didn't have much pain. She then said goodbye.

I got to see Mark too. He was sitting in a wheelchair by the door waiting for me. They had to shave a big section of his hair to stitch him up. The truck frame cut into his head, but the seatbelt kept him from falling out and saved him. He was all smiles and said he gets to leave as the only damage was superficial but wanted to wait to see me. He told me that Dad was on his way to them.

I cried hard this time, so relieved and grateful. I couldn't use either of my arms, so the tears just fell to the sides of my face and pooled in my ears and in the neck brace behind my head.

It was the bumpiest, most uncomfortable ride ever. Every bump shot new heights of pain through me. Without the worry for my siblings occupying my mind, I was now fully aware of my pain. I remained quiet and still. When we finally arrived, they took me back for immediate surgery. There were so many people in this cold and bright room. A man stood over me and told me he was putting a mask on my face that would make the pain go away. He pressed it over my mouth and nose, telling me to count backwards from ten. I said ten, smiled, and was gone.

***

I am now in a big, private, dark room. Jack, Emma, and my best friend are there waiting for me with a card and flowers from church friends. A nurse came in to let me know that I would be going in for a second surgery at 8:00 p.m.. She said the first one was a debridement to remove the glass and gravel from the road, and the second would be to close it with skin grafting. I couldn't feel much of anything right now and was happy about that. No pain at all.

She emphasized no food or water, asked how tall I was, and if I could be pregnant. I answered her questions, 5'5", and no, and she left. I was tired, and slowly everyone went home and it was just me staring at the seconds hand on the clock on the wall in front of my bed.

I was woken up by my dad and brother Ben. I asked where Ben came from, and he laughed because I didn't know he was at the university near where Dad was visiting. We had been living in the same state, and neither of us had any idea. I hadn't heard from him since our parents' divorce. We visited for a bit, and they gave me great updates on Mark and Claire. Finally, Dad leaned over and kissed my cheek and said he would be back after the next surgery. They left me to the clock.

All the pain was back, plus more from them digging through my leg to get all the glass and gravel out. I was hungry and so parched but told nothing by mouth until after my surgeries. I had been alone for hours now, other than a couple of nurses poking their heads in. The clock hands and the memory of the magic mask kept me going.

Finally, it was my time! It was about ten minutes to eight, and I thought they would come at any moment. I was now watching the door. Every second felt like an eternity, but no one came. I didn't want to bother anyone and knew that they were probably busy, so I kept waiting. The door was not opening. The clock was eight agonizing minutes past the hour, and I decided that I would hit the nurse button. But I couldn't reach it. It was dangling off the bed to my left. I couldn't bend that arm as it was wrapped from my forearm to my bicep. I couldn't reach over with my right arm as my wrist and hand were wrapped, and with my leg high in the air, I would roll off the bed trying.

Tears started to well up as I felt helpless and forgotten. I reached over with my face trying to see if I could grab the cord with my teeth but only hurt myself more in the attempts.

Twelve minutes passed the hour, and a nurse finally came in. I couldn't hold back any longer as tears fell. I told her how I couldn't reach the bell and that it was time, and I begged her to take me. She walked around my bed and was resting the call button near my hand but suddenly stepped back and froze. She said, "Didn't your father talk to you?" I said yes and that he would see me after the surgery. She quickly moved for the door and said she would be right back. She lied.

Twenty minutes after she left, another woman came in with the nurse following her but staying close to the door. She said she was a social worker and that this surgery required a guardian to sign first for payment. My father had pleaded with the hospital as he had no insurance and no money, but he did have a friend who was a surgeon and thought he would do this surgery for him pro bono. He said he was going to reach out to him and let the hospital know. They had not heard back.

They both left the room saying they would reach out to him. The social worker returned saying that no one could reach him but they contacted Ben as he left his number too. Ben said he was on his way. I thought I might die from the pain alone. The nurse needed to wait to hear back before asking for any pain medication.

Ben came into my room sometime later, the nurse following him, and I asked him where Dad was. Ben said he dropped him off at a singles dance and would be picking him up when my surgery was over.

My dad left me in pain to go to a dance, knowing that I was expecting surgery that wouldn't happen. Ben didn't believe me until the nurse confirmed what I shared. Ben didn't know what Dad did but the nurses asked him to talk with them outside of my room. My body was in shock. Not from the pain this time but from anger.

Ben ended up giving them my mom's number, and they reached her in California. All I was told was that there would be no surgery tonight, so they could give me water and food and something for the pain. The nurse told me to eat a little first, and I took a couple of bites of a banana, and then she handed me a little cup with a pill inside. I felt it slide down and hit my empty stomach and come right back up. I hated to throw up but even more when I couldn't wipe my own face. She offered me another one, but I just wanted to sleep now.

I was wakened by my dad and Ben about 11:00 p.m. I asked him why he bothered to come knowing what he did. He played dumb and said he didn't understand, so I said that they told me he was going to find a doctor but left for a dance. He got defensive and said I shouldn't believe my mom. What? The social worker told me this! They were asked to leave as visiting hours were over.

The following morning, the pain was just too much. When the nurse came in, I said I was ready to try another pain pill. Again, the moment it hit my stomach, it came right back up. Even with her helping to wipe my face, I couldn't get rid of the taste in my throat and in my nose. I was done with those.

There was a commotion outside of my room and I distinctly heard my dad's voice, Jack, and Bill! Emma came into the room, and I asked what was going on. She said that my mom and Bill were here, and they were fighting with my dad. Security was escorting them out of the hospital, and that she and Jack were leaving.

My mind was racing. Why were they here? I didn't ever want to see them again. After some time passed, Mom and Bill came into my room. Mom stood to my right, looking over my body and reaching out to run her fingers through my hair to try and brush it, but I pulled away. Bill was pacing at the foot of my bed. They said they couldn't believe that my dad sent me to live with these people and how mad Mom was that they took me in. Bill added that they were responsible for putting all of us kids in danger. I snapped back at them that why would they care anyway, as they were the first to get rid of me.

Things didn't go well from there, and a nurse came in, hearing the exchanges. With her in the room, Mom let me know that she knew my good-for-nothing father wouldn't have insurance on us, even though the judge ordered him to have it. That she had us all covered under her insurance and they had come to take me back with them to California.

Accommodations were made to transport me on a stretcher, and a nurse would be flying back with us, and I would have my surgery there. I was shocked and said I would not be going back with them ever! Lots of screaming took place, and my mom said, "fine!" and went to leave. Bill glared at me, said some things, and smacked my foot on his way out behind her.

SIX

That was the end of my visitors. I was angry and hurt and in pain, which kept me plenty occupied for the next couple of hours when a shift nurse came in to let me know that my surgery would be in the late afternoon. I asked how, and she let me know that my mom signed for it before leaving. Yes! I asked for the expected time and for the nurse button and began my new clock vigilance watch.

They were early by four minutes this time, and I was more excited than I can remember ever being. Involuntary tears flowed down my cheeks. With orderlies pushing in a new stretcher, the doctor was telling me what to expect. He explained that they would slice layers of skin from my butt, stretching it out in a machine which will punch holes in it, and stapling it to try and close my leg. He spoke of rejection and risks involved.

I laughed to think of what my butt on my leg would look like, but I was most concerned with how I would sit or lie on the new wound. My backside was the only place I could be in this broken body. There wasn't enough skin to take from my stomach, so he offered the outside of my thigh instead, and I quickly agreed.

The mask. Oh, how I dreamed of this mask and how I got to float away with no more pain. When I woke up this time, I thought I was dead. I woke in a white room lined with beds touching each other, with still bodies covered in white sheets up to the shoulders. No one was moving. I didn't hurt at all and figured I was in some holding room in heaven. I tried to sit up, forgetting that everything was wrapped, limiting my movement. So I just lay there, looking at the ceiling, thanking God to be out of pain.

Well, it wasn't heaven, but the hospital's recovery room. I woke up before they expected me to. They wheeled me back to my room, where orderlies picked me up by the sheets and moved me to my bed again. Two nurses gave me orders to keep my leg elevated high on the ramp they built and told me to stay as still as I could and try to sleep.

They warned that the pain would be much sharper after this surgery and would come back with pain meds before it wore off. I insisted that I didn't want that pill that made me throw up. Welcoming the sleep while there was no pain, I quickly fell into the rest I needed.

Awakened by someone calling my name, I slowly opened my eyes to see Jace there laying flowers on the desk beside me. That girl came with him and was standing in the doorway. Before I could even decide if I was angry or not, he was escorted out for the nurse change and vitals check. I was embarrassed that she could see what he did to my heartbeat.

You would think the pain would be in my leg, and it was, but not as much as the pain on my outer thigh where they took the skin. It was all I could feel! The nurse pulled back my covers to check it, and I looked down to see a big square of bloodiness covered with clear tape.

The next day, I woke in horror. I felt so much wetness under me, and when I looked down, I saw blood on the blanket coming from beneath me. I must have started my period. I begged God for mercy. I couldn't go to the bathroom on my own, and I didn't want this now. I called for the nurse, and she tried to assure me that it wasn't a big deal for them and she would get me cleaned up. I was so embarrassed.

On the third day, I warned the new nurse that I was on my cycle. When she was done cleaning things up and put extra padding under me, she said it looked like it was coming from my thigh and not my period after all. I was incredibly relieved.

The doctor had come in at the end of her telling me this and let me know that with such trauma, it may take my body months to a year to get back on a regular cycle. Good! I couldn't take myself to the bathroom and didn't have use of my hands to wash up. This was great news.

My in-hospital physical therapy started and consisted of being placed in a net which was lifted high and carried me across the ceiling of a huge room landing me in a hot tub. It hurt so terribly bad to have hot water forced into and around my leg. Not to mention how gross it was when they lifted me out and I felt my own skin and slime all over me.

After eight days in the hospital, the staples were removed and quite painful to feel, but I also watched them as they didn't put me out for this. The tool looked like three-pronged pliers, and I thought counting them as they came out might help with the pain. Instead, I was just shocked at how many there were holding my skin together, praying that my skin wouldn't just split open. The anticipation of each one to be removed and the actual pull hurt the same.

It's been a month since the accident. School had started, so my friends were gone, but I was bedbound. On the way to one of my doctor appointments, Jack stopped by the junkyard to show me the truck. It was a mangled mess that clearly rolled a couple of times with only one tire. He let me know that he was working on getting the truck back. I didn't understand.

I was still broken up over Jace. I dreamed that he would come over, but I couldn't wash my hair or get dressed, and if he saw me again, I wanted him to regret hurting me. I was in no shape to be looked at. My heart hurt even worse now that I couldn't distract myself, stuck on this couch alone.

Since I couldn't walk, Jack and Emma didn't want me downstairs as it was easier if I was on the pullout in the living room. My friends came often after school and on the weekends, and I stayed busy on the phone trying to manage my doctor appointments, to thank people for flowers and meals, and to try and get homeschooling set up. I was stir crazy, not being able to move and not having any privacy. Ever.

The mail was left on the coffee table next to the pullout, and I saw an opened letter from the police and read it when everyone was asleep. It was a ticket for them due to bald, blistered, and re-tread tires with patches that caused the accident. That the tread was just gone on the three tires during that drive. I never said anything to them about it, and they never said anything to me.

It had become too much for Jack and Emma to try and care for me while fighting with my parents. My dad was threatening to sue them, and my mom and Bill were calling and sending letters they would write about some insurance payment. I agreed that this wasn't fair to them and relented in going back. Mom and Bill drove out this time, and I was headed back to California in a van. I cried to leave my friends. They were the only family I had.

The whole of the conversations revolved around my terrible father and those horrible people for taking me and hurting me and my siblings. If I wasn't sleeping, I was pretending to be so I didn't have to respond. They were in a different house with just Olivia, Mom, Bill, and me now. I learned that not long after they sent me away, they also sent his son away. They started with five kids and got rid of three.

Bill had to carry me upstairs, and there was no way to manage the turns without banging my leg many times. I admit that I was looking forward to a private room that I could hide in. There was nothing else I was looking forward to anymore.

At night, I managed to slowly drop off the side of the bed and crawl backwards, dragging my leg from my bedroom to the bathroom with the elbow of the 'good' arm. Sometimes I would be so tired that I would fall asleep on the bathroom floor, not able to make it back but happy to be able to do this on my own finally. I was very careful not to upset anyone. I couldn't run if I wanted to.

Food would be brought up to me, and I felt ravished, always asking for seconds. Bill took pride in his cooking and really liked that I always asked for more. Apparently, every state was having issues with the home-school programs and funding. I felt like I was in fifth grade again with the curriculum. My new doctor was pushing me to try and walk. I didn't know how that could happen because the rush of blood to my leg still high above my head was throbbing and excruciating.

Mom was able to rent a wheelchair with a right leg rest where I would place many pillows to elevate my leg. I was starting a new school again as the home school option wasn't working. The classrooms were definitely not set up for wheelchairs with a leg sticking out. Plus, I had to do a few bandage changes during school. It was really gross, and people would come around to watch the freak show.

I am now about four months after the accident. Even though they said there were skin grafts, under the bandages, it sure looked raw and open. It took me a long time to get ready and slink down the stairs for a ride to school each morning. It was getting close to the Thanksgiving break, and I was now able to lower my leg for brief moments and walk a couple of steps with crutches before the pain was too much.

We had gotten into a routine now. Mom had me drive her to work, and then I would go to school, pick her up for lunch, and then again after work. She had been running me around so much these last months, and I was happy to give her a break. Bill was very clear about the strict rules and that I had better not step out of line even once. I did occasionally see him following me or show up at my school or at the house to make sure I was where he expected me. I had no friends and could only move a little at a time. Where was I going to go?

With Christmas near, this was the last week before the holiday break for school. This morning, I was on the floor in front of my closet after I had wrapped my leg, working to pull on my pants. I couldn't button them. I knew I was being fed well here and definitely ate more than my share. I reached for a different pair of pants when I felt a jump.

I sat perfectly still, but nothing. What was that?

I was running late now and had to hurry, so I dressed and got downstairs. I couldn't shake that feeling, though.

SEVEN

Could I? Was that...? I started to count the months since I was with Jace, noting that I did have to get up to the bathroom several times at night, my pants weren't fitting, and I still didn't have my period. But that jump. I hadn't felt anything since, but I've never felt anything like that before and needed to know. I didn't have any money and didn't have any friends. I also couldn't take the risk that Bill wouldn't follow me if I drove to a store.

For days, I was sick just thinking about how to get a test without them knowing. Although Bill was being kind, I feared him. He told me often that one step out of line and I would be gone, and I knew not to doubt his threat. I finally decided that I had no way to do this on my own and I had to tell my mom that I might be. She would be so angry and disappointed. She might kick me out, but I didn't know what else to do. Bill reminded me daily that I had to earn his trust. I didn't know what would happen if I upset him.

I tried to reason that the only signs of pregnancy were the one-time jump I felt, if that was real, and no period. I just couldn't stop the nagging inside me. I decided that I would tell Mom when she was napping at the lunch break, only if I knew Bill wouldn't be there. I had practiced and made myself sick for days thinking about what the response would be. I could see her being so upset that this might be it for me, and I would have to figure out where to go. Mom had her back to me while she was resting, so I sat close behind her so she didn't have room to turn around and face me. With a racing heart and sick stomach, I said, "Mom, I think I might be pregnant."

She was able to flip around completely alert with a piercing stare. After some initial shock and rapid-fire questions, she told me not to say anything to anyone until we know for sure. This wasn't the first time I talked to her about Jace. She was so disgusted with me and my Dad and the family that took me in. She warned me not to say anything to anyone.

The next day at lunch, she had set an appointment for me, and we drove there together. I peed in a cup, and they drew my blood, now sitting in the waiting room. Mom wouldn't look at or talk to me.

We were called back to an exam room with a nurse and the doctor. They did an ultrasound, and the room was quiet. No one was talking. The doctor looked to my mom and told her I was pregnant, it was a boy, about five months along, and he didn't expect the baby to live based on the conversation he had with the hospital, my surgeries, and months of pain medication. That if he lived, there likely would be missing or undeveloped body parts and brain function.

Mom gasped and cried. I told them that I never took the pain meds as they made me throw up, but the doctor didn't believe me and said I wouldn't have been able to handle the pain. They didn't respond to me, and the way they looked at each other told me they didn't believe me. The nurse rested a wand on my stomach, and we listened to this swishing rhythm. His heartbeat!

As we left the office, all eyes were on me, but no one spoke. I couldn't walk without assistance, and even though my leg was throbbing, I didn't want to stop. It took forever to get out of there. Mom and I sat in the car for over an hour. She was so angry with me. Lots of questions were fired in my direction, but mostly how to tell Bill. Her fear of his reaction matched mine, which wasn't reassuring. Mom decided that she would tell him tonight, but I needed to leave and get as far from the house as I could until she came to get me. She couldn't promise that he would let me return and to be prepared for that.

That evening after dinner, Mom looked at me, and I knew it was time. I had packed a bag with some clothes and bandages for my leg, grabbed my crutches, and went out the front door. I still was only able to handle about six or so steps before the pain and pressure was too much, and I had to sit and elevate my leg, but I felt panic through my entire body to go as fast and as far as I could before she told him.

I spent this time dreaming of this child. I had always loved children and knew what kind of mother I wanted to be. I knew of the conditional love I felt and would make sure my children would always have unconditional love and know that I wanted them so badly. I don't know how long I was out, but I remember it getting dark and thinking that it can't be good that I'm still here waiting.

Sometime later, both of them were driving around looking for me. I saw their car and stood up so they could see me. I was so sick to my stomach. They pulled up to the curb nearby but didn't look at me or say anything, so I hobbled over and got in the backseat.

Back at the house, we all sat in the living room while I was talked to death about the type of person I had become. That I had shamed the family and embarrassed my mother. Then Bill asked me what I was going to do. I said that I was going to get stronger so that when he is born, I can get a job and take care of him. Bill asked where I would live, and I froze. I guess I had hoped that I could live there for a while until I could walk and have the means to get an apartment. This was something they must have talked about before coming to get me, as they had already decided.

Bill started by telling me that they are not raising my son, and if I chose to keep him, I would have to find another place to live. I was tearful but replied that I would live in a shelter if I had to. Mom said that if I lived in a shelter and couldn't provide for myself or him, they would take him away and put him in a home, and I would never know where and wouldn't see him again. I told them that I still loved Jace, and if he knew, his family would help us.

Bill told me to go to my room, and they would talk more. About an hour later, they came upstairs to say they agreed that I could tell Jace but that Bill would be on the line also.

I was in my room, and Bill dialed the number from the kitchen. When the phone picked up, he barked out to speak to Jace. Feeling sick to my stomach doesn't come close to explaining how I felt. Bill told Jace who he was and that I needed to speak with him and that he needed to listen.

I just blurted out to Jace that I was pregnant. He was silent. No reply. Then Bill got angry and yelled his name. He said, "Yes, sir," and went on to explain that there is another girl also pregnant, and he needs time to decide who to marry. I quickly said, "You don't have a choice; she can have you. Do you want to know anything about the baby?" He said no. I replied, "You are either all in or all out of the baby's life." He said he was out and hung up. I cried tears that must have depleted all the strength I had and crumpled on the floor of my room.

Bill and Mom came upstairs a few minutes later, and I could see their pity. Bill let me know that he called back and spoke with his mom. She said something not kind about me and hung up after saying they knew Jace couldn't be the father.

I begged them to please let me stay with my baby, and we wouldn't make a noise, wouldn't ask for any other help, and would get on my feet as quickly as possible to move out. They said absolutely not, and it wouldn't be discussed again.

Sleepless nights trying to wrap my head around this little boy, the accident, not taking any pain meds because I hated to throw up, and the miracle he could have survived through it all. I remembered when the nurse came into the room with my best friend and guardians and asked if I might be pregnant. How I quickly said no. I didn't think I was, but I certainly wasn't going to admit it was possible with them in the room. I was never asked again.

I didn't have any question that my baby would be okay. If I hadn't gotten in the accident, I would have known I was pregnant a long time ago and be the one marrying Jace. Thoughts that I would have nowhere to live, couldn't walk still, and didn't want social services to take him away. I thought about adoption. I knew there were people that couldn't have children and that I could at least choose the family who could give him what I couldn't and Jace wouldn't.

I didn't want this but decided that it was the best decision for him and the only one for me. I prayed telling God what I decided, which was to let me have this little boy, find a perfect home for him, and then let him take me. I picked out his name. Ren Scott, my nephew's and brother's middle names.

The next morning I apologized to Mom and Bill and thanked them for letting me live there. That I would find a family for him and asked if I could stay until he was born. They agreed with conditions. Mom said that I would hide out so no one knew, and they both said that I wasn't going to freeload off of them and would earn my keep. I gladly agreed and became a maid and cook. Bill was very strict on the housecleaning rules so much so that the vacuum lines were not to have any of my footsteps in them. I worked every day to clear the backyard forest of weeds of their new home, being careful not to expose my leg to the hot sunshine dragging it beside me, while I rushed to finish school.

I refused to be a high school dropout and wanted my diploma before he was born. I was so far behind in school that I didn't know how to make this happen. I just didn't want those to be the descriptions he would be told of his mother.

EIGHT

All I did was study and make sure Mom and Bill didn't regret letting me stay or change their minds. I lived with the fear that they would and I didn't know what I would do.

One of the opportunities in my rapid studies was a discussion with a group of teen parents, people who had been adopted, and parents that had adopted. The most impactful messages for me were those where the adoptive parents told the children, or didn't tell the children. The grown children that were placed for adoption and their thoughts on how it impacted their lives and what they wished was different.

I heard of children that knew from the beginning, those who stayed in touch with the birth family, those who waited until the children were adults to tell, and those who never told. The one now grown child who was told as an adult felt that he was lied to and grew distant from his parents because of it. He said that he understood they tried to give him a normal, secure life by withholding that, but it really hurt him, and he was struggling with his identity now.

The OB heard of my plan to find a home, and he gave me the number of his friends that were quite wealthy and unable to have children themselves. I met them. They had a lot of questions about ethnicity, family history, and Jace. I didn't get any warm feelings but figured that was because I didn't want to let him go. I told them that. I told them that I wanted more than anything else to keep him but couldn't find a way. I made them promise to send me pictures. They definitely had all the things I didn't have to offer Ren.

Feeling Ren grow inside me was so amazing, and heart-wrenching. I kept hoping I would find a way, Mom and Bill would change their mind or some great miracle would come before he did.

Six schools in three states in three and a half years, and just before my due date, I graduated with my high school diploma with a 4.2 GPA. My high school had helped me find an accelerated school. I could go at my own pace, but if I got anything below a B on any test or assignment, I would be kicked out and would have no other choice but my GED or return to traditional school.

Almost Easter, and I was overdue by a week. The doctor scheduled me the next morning to be induced at the hospital. Mom's insurance allowed me up to three days, so I asked for every single hour with him and without the couple. They didn't need to induce after all. When I arrived, they said I was in labor. It felt like he was turning, and my stomach was tight, but I didn't know this was labor. Within four hours of arriving at the hospital and two pushes, he was here.

This little tiny boy with dark hair came so fast. He was completely perfect in every way. I held him, couldn't keep my eyes off him, trying to burn his sweet face in my memory so I would never forget. Mom, Bill, Grandma, and Olivia were there too. I was begging God for some answer on how to not let him go and wondered if I were to sneak out with him, where I could go without him being taken from me. Maybe they would fall in love with him too and not let him go.

The last day came too soon. My eyes burned from the stinging tears and excruciating pain throughout my entire soul that this was it. My family gathered around as I dressed him and was told the couple had arrived.

When the nurse came to take Ren, I struggled to breathe and fell to the floor. I was lifted to a wheelchair and pushed down to the car. Crying uncontrollably. We passed the nurses' station, and they had all gathered and were crying too. I begged God to take me and make this pain go away. It felt like my broken heart was crushing my lungs, and I couldn't breathe. Nor did I want to.

The ride home was not even ten minutes. Bill went out to mow the lawn, and I remember thinking how heartless he was acting as if nothing had happened. I didn't make it far inside the house and collapsed on the couch, pressing my face into the cushion to block out the world.

Within thirty minutes, Mom and Bill came to me and said they wanted their grandson back!! I threw myself into their arms and ran to the car.

***

Ren was the most wonderful baby. He never really cried, and even in the middle of the night, only gave out a small whimper when he was hungry. I was anxiously anticipating any need he had and also wanting to make sure he didn't disturb Bill. The complete joy I felt every moment, so happy to have him in my arms. He slept next to me in a laundry basket, carefully wrapped and so very cherished.

There were very strict rules set to make sure we didn't disrupt the home. I was still shaky when it came to walking but was so much stronger now. Without a job, I committed to taking care of the needs of their home to earn my keep. I wish I could do more. I looked at jobs and apartments to rent, but it would take me working three jobs to just make rent, and I would never see Ren. This was on my mind as I knew my time there was limited.

I was no longer in hiding, and Ren was proudly on display with the neighbors and church. So many wonderful people donated a stroller, car seat, and clothing. The support was heartwarming. I loved this little bundle like I'd never loved before. Almost three months later, Bill came home early from work completely broken. He didn't say anything to me but just went into his room and shut the door. Mom also came home early, and they stayed locked away for hours. I could hear some faint crying. I later learned that his company had re-organized and many were let go. Including him. Over the next days and weeks, I overheard their concerns about finances.

News came that three of my siblings were coming for a visit: Mark, Claire, and Ben. I hadn't heard or seen them since the accident, but I knew Mom told them about the baby. I learned that Mark was also placed in a foster situation after the accident.

I wasn't allowed to use the phone long-distance, so I had no contact with anyone. The one brother that did not come, Byron, was still in Colorado. He was the sibling I got along with best, but we hadn't seen or heard from each other in over a year. It was his son that I named Ren after.

I was happy to see them all and loved sharing little silly Ren with them. He was four months old now and had the sweetest personality and unforgettable laughter. He never lost any hair, but it went from dark to very light. He was the sunshine of my life.

I felt their heavy judgement and stayed small, feeling my own shame, often hearing conversations about me but not to me. Byron was brought on the speaker phone to say hello to everyone that night. This was the first he heard about Ren and insisted that I should come back to Colorado and we could raise our boys together. That I could stay with him and he would help watch Ren so I could work. Bill didn't like this and firmly told him to stop.

Ben, Claire, and Mark were leaving the next morning. Although they didn't live in Colorado, Ben and Mark were heading there to visit Dad. I was up all night thinking about what Byron said. I didn't want to leave Mom, Olivia, and Bill, but I was a financial burden on them and couldn't afford to live on my own in California. I did love the idea of the little boys being raised together and adored Byron. By morning, I had decided that I would ask to get a ride back with them.

As hard as Bill was on me, I think I broke both his and Mom's hearts with my plan to leave. Little Ren had stolen every heart. I just felt like this was my opportunity to step up and make a life for us. Ben was hesitant as there wasn't a lot of room in the car but agreed, and I got busy packing everything I could for the long drive. So many tears fell and promises were made of visits back.

I felt this ongoing judgement on the drive back. They would barely speak to me and didn't have much interest in Ren. I stayed focused on what this new life could hold for us, and told myself I was just here for the ride. We only had one big stop, which was with a family Ben knew who had invited us all for dinner near the university he was attending. Most of the dinner, I was outside walking Ren, who was struggling to sleep with the change to his normal routine.

Ben and the man of the house had come out to grab something from the car and were not shy about saying unkind things about a girl like me, knowing I could hear them. They said I had no right keeping a child I couldn't provide for. I made sure to stay outside and away from everyone until we left and didn't talk unless it was required the rest of the drive.

Ren was so cute and did incredibly well even being cooped up and strapped into the car seat. I was upset watching my siblings practically ignore that we were in the car but kept focus that they wouldn't be in our lives once we arrived. Ren and I quietly played games and I would softly sing silly songs to him. I didn't want him to feel the tension I was feeling. When he was able to sleep, I would pretend to also but my mind was so active trying to imagine the new life we would be creating.

The judgement I felt on the drive was nothing compared to what was to come. The world seemed to feel the same. I know I was young but looked much younger, so that didn't help. So many hardships were felt as I navigated a cold world, but I didn't care because I had the warmth from my little Ren. He was my world and my only focus.

NINE

It took a little time, and the struggle was painful and difficult, but I managed to get my own apartment in the same complex as Byron. His situation became unstable, so I had found a woman to watch Ren when I worked. I found her number on a grocery store billboard, and when I met with her, she just took right to Ren. She had a nice house and lived with her elderly mother and her daughter, who was a couple of years older than me. The three women just loved on and spoiled him. I remember the daughter telling me that people thought she was his mother because they looked so much alike. I laughed because they both were very blonde with brown eyes and had rolls in their thighs.

It took me three buses to get him there and me to work every day, but I was happy to have our own place. It was a harsh winter, and I really wanted to make sure he was warm as we walked to the bus stops. I had him wrapped so well that he couldn't move, but his chubby little cheeks and bright eyes were always smiling and happy. I never knew love could be this fierce. He was all I thought about.

Months into this job, something stopped me in my tracks, hearing a very firm voice say, "GET REN!". It was my voice! I heard it again and again. I didn't have a car, so I ran over to my friend Bert (his name was Ernie) and told him I needed his truck. I had never asked before, but he could see something desperate in my request and just reached into his pocket and tossed me the keys.

I ran out to the truck and sped into the neighborhood down the road, feeling a panic in me to hurry. When I got a house away from the babysitter, I could see the daughter's car in the driveway with Ren in his car seat and her backing out onto the street. I jumped out and ran to his door, pulling him out the open window, car seat and all. I just stood there looking at her. They had permission to take Ren out and often did, but there was something that told me this was different, but I had no words and just stared at her, looking for an answer.

She just stared right back, frozen. I looked into the car and could see suitcases and bags filling every space. I slowly backed away, trying to make sense of what this all meant, then turned and ran for the truck. I didn't even buckle Ren in but drove back to work and ran inside straight to Bert. When I told him what happened, he called the cops. I was shaking but just wanted to play with Ren and make sure he wasn't hurt or scared.

I was later told that the daughter wasn't there when the cops arrived, but they spoke to her mom and grandmother, who shared that she had shown them a written letter from me asking her to take care of Ren as I wasn't able to provide for him. That she was going to live with her boyfriend in Nebraska and raise him.

The cops had now come to my work to take a report. The memories of things she had said about Ren looking like her, and she hoped to have a baby, and how much she loved Ren started flashing through my mind. I had been so caught up in survival, I didn't see the red flags in front of me.

Terrified of ever leaving Ren again, I quit my job and worked a schedule out with Byron as he was the only one I could trust. With Byron's schedule, I needed to work late nights. During the day, I would be with Ren and my nephew.

I never could pay the startup fee for the utilities, so the lights and heat never worked. Water was included in my rent. My apartment door was inside a hallway and across from the laundry room, which they kept too hot. I propped my door and the laundry door open, which heated my place pretty well. We got light from the hallway, and if we needed more, we would play and eat at the folding table next door.

I didn't eat much and made sure Ren had everything he needed. Someone gave us a crib, but I would find that Ren had paint chips in his mouth from teething on the rail, so I tossed it, and we slept on the floor together. Mom sent a box of food once.

Most were cans, but I didn't have a can opener or any pot or dishes to heat things up in. That would be for next month's paycheck.

It was hard for me to adjust to working nights, but I preferred this as Ren was headed to bed for the night when I left, and I was there in the morning. We spent a lot of time at the library. It was warm, and there were toys and books. I read him every story. Ren couldn't get enough. Things were really hard, but I had never been happier still. At the new job, I worked with some fun people, and after close, they would often just hang out for a couple of hours. Since Ren was asleep and I didn't pick him up until morning, I would stay for a little.

A guy named Eric was always cracking jokes and never sat still. He goofed off and pranked everyone. I couldn't help but laugh, and it felt good to not feel the weight of life. The guys took turns walking the girls out when they were leaving to make sure they got to their cars safely. I didn't have a car and didn't want anyone to know, so I always gave excuses that I didn't need any help or I would go to the restroom and then sneak out before they knew I was leaving. I didn't like to talk about myself, so when questions would come my way, I was good at turning the question on them so they could share more about themselves.

One of those nights, Eric followed me out. He didn't ask to walk me to my car, which is what I expected. He was definitely flirting and saying I seemed shy, but he wanted to hear more about me. We stood out front for about thirty minutes talking when I couldn't stop yawning and said I needed to get home. He only asked if he could give me a ride home. He must have known that I didn't have a car. It was winter and really cold out with the wind. I accepted and had him pull near where Byron lived and jumped out quickly, thanking him. I didn't want to give him a chance to ask to come in.

These rides became more frequent. Everyone seemed to know that when I left, Eric would too. I really liked him, and he wasn't shy to let me know he was interested. I did tell him I had a baby, and he didn't seem to care. He didn't ask about him, but it didn't seem to bother him. The time we spent together was after work, so I didn't have Ren with me.

A week after the rides started, he asked if I'd come to his place to hang out the next day as we both had it off. I let him know that I would like that, but I'd have Ren with me. He asked if I could get a babysitter, saying he wanted to date me and not my kid. That answer set something off in me. He didn't know what we had been through, but I got upset and just said, "If you go out with me, you go out with him too" and left. I was really upset and figured that is how all guys are going to feel. I didn't need to date anyway.

The next afternoon, Eric came by and said he had just made lunch for me and Ren and would we come with him. I didn't have a phone and didn't know he knew which apartment I was in so I was surprised to see him. I held the door so it was only open a crack as I didn't want him to see that I had no furniture.

I had mixed feelings from what he said before, but thought I put him in a hard place, and now that he had time to think about it, he changed his mind. I told him we would need a minute and shut the door on him. Grabbing some of Ren's favorite toys, we left. I was excited for the date.

I am not bragging, but Ren is the best little guy ever. Everyone loved being around him as he was just happy and easygoing. He rarely fussed, and if he did, I knew exactly what he needed. After lunch, I told Eric that Ren was about ready for a nap, so I sat down with him to rock him to sleep. Eric started to play a video game, and everyone seemed happy. It was so nice to not be alone and was happy that he got to see that Ren wasn't any trouble.

We were spending all our time together. Although Eric didn't hold Ren or play with him, he didn't seem bothered by him either. I tried to put myself in his position and was very patient but knew he would grow to adore this little guy. How could you not! The dreamer in me could already picture a family with him.

He got frustrated a couple of times when he wanted to do something I didn't want Ren to do and always refused a sitter. Once to a horror movie, and I said no. For two reasons really: because I didn't like horror movies, but I wasn't going to bring Ren. Eric decided to cut the date short and take us home. I knew he was upset, so on the drive home, I told him about the babysitter incident and that I would never leave Ren again. I felt Eric soften a little but could also see the storm in his eyes that this is how it would always be with me.

We didn't talk for a couple of days. I didn't know if things were over between us. I looked at the work schedule that was just posted and saw a shift we both worked the next night. I guess I would find out then.

It was like nothing had happened. There was no conversation about it, we spent all our time together again, and in Tina fashion, I was falling quickly for him. Eric had a roommate, and Ren didn't have a place to sleep away from everyone, so over time, Eric would stay with me. I didn't have any furniture except for an old mattress on my floor. Eric didn't say anything and didn't seem to care about much. I figured he was just an easygoing guy.

I was struggling to figure him out. Was he falling for me too or just happy with my company for now? I didn't push, as I was happy and hopeful. Especially on that day, we grabbed some sandwiches and went to a park. When I placed Ren in the swing, Eric actually came over also and started pretending like Ren would knock him over. Ren couldn't stop laughing, and it spurred Eric on. My eyes welled up so happy that they were playing together, and my hope for more.

Ren really was happy. I felt so grateful that he didn't seem to have taken on the hardship situation I placed him in. I moved to a different complex that included the utilities. Eric was now spending every day and night with us. He still had his other apartment, but we were something now. I'm not sure quite what, but I was sure in time, it would become more clear. Whenever I needed to bathe or care for Ren, Eric would play video games or leave.

TEN

Around Ren's first birthday, I met Eric's family. I could definitely feel the judgement and hear the quiet conversations of concern they had for Eric. I told him that I loved him, but he didn't respond. I finally got a phone and was able to get an old couch. Eric brought his TV over and video games, so I got an antenna allowing Ren to watch Sesame Street.

My mom called occasionally, and when she found out about Eric living with me, not saying he loved me, and not helping with rent, she was not happy. Bill would get on the phone and insist on talking with him, but I would always say he wasn't there. Mom told me he was taking the milk without caring for the cow or something like that and strongly expressed her disgust that I would be in this type of relationship outside of marriage. Hadn't she taught me better? Hadn't I learned my lesson? How could I do this to Ren? Saying if he loved me and had good intentions, he would marry me, and that I needed to tell him that if he wasn't going to marry me, that he needed to move out.

I avoided their calls as much as possible, but her words wouldn't stop nagging me. He had been living with me for six months now. I was scared to lose him and felt sure he would leave if I gave him the ultimatum. He would never say he loved me, and the only thing he had said was that he never saw himself married with kids.

Mom sent me some money so I could visit. I had already talked with Eric about wanting to visit and asked if he would come. We would have to drive as there was only enough money for Ren and me to fly. Mom and Bill made sure we slept in separate rooms, and I loved how they engulfed Ren with love and attention. I felt like the most proud mom showing him off. His personality was infectious. Tons of thick blonde hair with chubby cheeks and a huge smile. He started walking at eight months, so he was navigating their backyard easily, looking like a little man and not a baby. Grandma and Olivia were there too, just laughing and smiling. This, of course, made Ren do silly things to get more responses from his attentive audience.

Mom and Bill begged me to move back to California, but I was so happy living on my own and with Eric. As expected, Bill pulled Eric aside for a stern conversation. I warned him that it would happen, and Eric didn't seem phased.

The day we returned from the trip, after we unpacked and I got Ren down for the night, I told Eric that I needed him to decide. That if we weren't married, I didn't want to continue to live together, but we could still date. When Eric didn't respond to me, I told him that I felt he was using me and knew what I wanted but would never give it to me. So he looked over at me and, without much emotion, said he loved me and he would marry me. I jumped up so excited, hugging him, saying yes, and quickly called my mom.

    I was so happy and planning the wedding. I did ask him if he planned to adopt Ren and promised nothing would change. I would still do everything for him but wanted us all to have the same last name. Eric officially moved out of his other apartment. My funds were really limited, and he still wasn't paying for rent, but he told me once we were married he would. I was picking out songs and pricing little tuxedo rentals and trying on dresses at the local consignment boutique. Eric didn't have much interest in this, but everyone said that guys usually don't.

    His family was less than happy and would pull him aside, trying to talk him out of it. The religious difference we were raised in was also a problem for them. Neither Eric nor I cared, but his family sure did. His family never even went to church, so I was surprised it mattered to them. They wanted us to be married by a priest. I didn't care - I just wanted to marry Eric. There was a beautiful cathedral adjacent to the private school he graduated from, so we decided to do it there. It was magical with the high-pitched ceiling and colorful stained glass. I had never seen anything like it outside of movies. It seemed like the dream place to walk down the aisle.

A month before the scheduled date, the church required that we meet with the priest to get his blessing to continue. The meeting went fine until the end. We were presented with a contract that we were to sign that stated we agreed to raise our children in the church. Eric reached to sign. I was not Catholic and had no intention of raising Ren in their church. Eric was raised only attending Easter and Christmas, and I was not going to sign that. I said so. We were told that there isn't a follow-up and I just needed to sign if we were to marry there. I wouldn't do it. I refused to sign something in a chapel promising something I knew I wasn't going to do.

Keeping the date as it marked the one-year anniversary from the day we met, but not having enough time or money to switch locations, we agreed to go to the courthouse to make it legal and would plan something even bigger that next summer. I didn't want to wear my wedding dress for this and to save it for the big ceremony, so I pulled my favorite and only cocktail dress I had worn to an Air Force Academy ball about the time I met Eric.

The night before we were to be married, my church was having a Christmas party that we attended. It was a fun night with Santa and a big dinner. Ren was a year and a half now. I was excitedly telling everyone that we were to be married the next day. The Bishop and some friends pulled Eric and me aside and said we could save the $50 court fee and he would marry us there instead. There were plenty of leftovers from the Christmas dinner, and our friends and family could come also. There was a large classroom-type room we would use, and we said yes!

When we got home from dinner, Eric called his parents and brother to invite them. I didn't have anyone to invite. His dad and stepmom were the first call, happy for us and said they would be there. Everyone knew we were going to the courthouse, so it was only a surprise that we changed the location. They said not to call his brother as they wanted to surprise him. Then he called his mom.

She had been with me to pick out my dress months ago and was sweet with little Ren. Expecting her to be happy, but she was not. She told Eric to take her off the speaker phone, but I could still hear her. She got hysterical and believed I had tricked him and that he would now become a member of my church. She said she would not go and did not support us. Since I heard her, I was trying to tell Eric to tell her that there would be no conversion - just saving us some money and no different from the courthouse.

She was not having it, and Eric locked himself in the room with the phone while they kept talking. When he finally came out, he said the wedding was off as she refused to come. We fought late into the night and into the early hours of the morning. He wanted me to just sign the paper from the cathedral, and his family would be happy. I was not going to do that. It was much more than a paper to me. Eric finally agreed to marry me in the church as money was tight, and I assured him there would be nothing to sign like his church had.

We had an appointment to pick up my engagement ring the next morning that we had been making payments on, and then we would head over to the church. Eric couldn't believe his mom wouldn't come and tried calling her a few times, but she didn't pick up.

I put on my dress, and he and Ren put on button-up shirts and nice pants. My eyes were puffy and red from the night before. We went out to his car only to find that a tire was missing. Someone stole a tire off the car that night. We couldn't even put on a spare because they dropped the car, bending the rim. Eric called his dad, who quickly called for a car rental to pick us up for the day. We were now running late but picked up the pretty ring and headed for the church. We were late to our own wedding.

The church members had set up some tables with leftover Christmas decorations, lights, food, and dessert from the night before. It felt really special and was more than I had expected. Eric's dad and stepmother were greeted with Ren running into their arms, squealing with happiness. They scooped him up and loved on him. We both hoped his mom would have changed her mind and shown up, but she wasn't there.

Eric's brother and wife were there and apparently not happy about the surprise as they were not told what was going on until they arrived. When they did find out and saw that their mom wasn't there, they had the chance to get caught up on everything that happened with his mom before we arrived.

His brother met us at the door to the room everyone was gathered in and told Eric that they needed to speak right away. I wasn't included, but Eric told me that he didn't want us to get married, and he said that Eric could have twenty wives but only one mother, and he was disrespecting her by going through with this. While they were talking, I overheard his sister-in-law commenting loudly to his dad about my red dress and how fitting for me, and at least I didn't try to wear white. I started to cry, but Eric said his mom would get over it and come to the ceremony next summer, seeing that they didn't convert him. We went into the room together.

I tried to shake it off and was so happy to be getting married. Feeling both happy and sad at the same time was familiar to me. I loved Eric so much and wanted to be his wife. The ceremony didn't last long. I could see his brother and sister-in-law pouting in the corner. Not showing any support and talking during the entire five-minute service, saying things like the tire missing was a sign that we ignored to not marry. Although his brother wasn't too friendly with me in the year before this, his sister-in-law made sure I knew that I was not welcome, so I hadn't expected much from them anyway. Whenever we had been together that previous year, she would just look me up and down with her arms crossed, showing her disapproval. A woman who helped set up the food took a couple of photos, and I was so glad because they were the only ones taken that day.

When we got home, we were all tired and laid down to take a nap. I assumed the celebration would continue after we rested. We woke up, and Eric went straight for the video games. I made food and played with Ren. Eric could get lost in games for twelve hours or more, but I was sure he wouldn't today.

Early evening came, and I passively mentioned that maybe we could go out to dinner and then drive around looking at Christmas lights. He didn't look up, but about an hour later, turned off the video games. I went into the room and got Ren and me dressed up warmly for the night out. When we came back out, a football game was playing, and I could tell he wasn't planning to go anywhere.

I was mad but only asked to borrow his keys so Ren and I could go celebrate. Some back-and-forth arguing, and Eric grabbed a jacket and came with us. We did go to dinner, and even the waitress said she was surprised to hear this was our wedding night. Everyone could see that Eric was not thrilled to be there.

The big ceremony never happened. His family would not come, and my mom now said that since we were already married, they wouldn't come either. I was the only one who wanted it. As hurt as I was, I had always seen myself married with children, so I just focused on how grateful I was.

ELEVEN

Now that we were married, I went down to the courthouse and asked how to move forward with the adoption. They asked to see Ren's birth certificate and said that if I hadn't put Jace's name down as the father, it would have been easier, but with his name, he would have to sign a legal document saying that he agreed. I knew he would.

I called the number of Jace's parents' house, and luckily he was still living there. I told him that I was married and needed him to sign relinquishment papers in front of a notary. He said he would and to mail the form to him. I heard a little child in the background and knew that would be the other child he had. It was the sound of a little girl.

I was excited for the adoption. When weeks passed with nothing returned in the mail, I called him again. A young female voice answered, and when I asked to speak with Jace, she wanted to know who I was and why I was calling. I told her my name and that I was waiting for Jace to sign the papers and return them, but they still hadn't arrived. She began to cry and asked when I spoke with him. She cried saying that Jace had promised all along that the baby wasn't his. She asked a couple of questions about when Ren was born and got hysterical and hung up.

Two days later and very late at night, Jace called to tell me that he wasn't going to sign. His parents had him speak with an attorney, and they didn't believe that I was going to let him off that easy. They said that if he signed the papers, it would be admitting that he was the father. Then he told me to never call there again and hung up. I thought how stupid he was, as he would legally be off the hook if he signed the paper.

Back to the courthouse to explain what happened and what to do next. I was told that I had to post an ad in the local paper (my local paper, even though he was in another state) listing the court date and opportunity to appear. It had to run for a certain time frame, so I did what they said and waited out the clock. We went to the courthouse, a few questions were asked by the judge, and the papers were signed.

Two more children came, and I adored my little family and loved being their mom. I still wanted more, but I had some complications with my last and couldn't have been happier. Being a mom was magical and exactly what I wanted for my life. I made a lot of promises to myself that my children wouldn't experience the things I did and that they would be loved and cherished. I would never play favorites and would always put their needs before mine.

I asked many times for help with the little ones, as three kids five and under was a lot, and without looking up, Eric made jokes that I was the one who wanted kids. That was true. With Ren, I never expected or asked for any help with him. He was my son. It just continued with little Trafton and sweet Jessica. I so needed to have the happy family, so I ignored his joke and accepted that the babies were my responsibility. I was happy caring for and loving on them. They were my world and taught me a love that has never been surpassed.

There were many happy times as a family. Really. We took on the traditional roles where he would go to work and I would do everything else. When Eric was home, we made sure it was playtime. He would engage more when we were being silly or playing games. When we weren't able to make ends meet, I also worked.

The expectation that the wife does the work in the home never changed. I would come home after working overnight only to be faced with a mess of a house, and the only thing he managed to do was keep the kids alive. Baths, laundry, and toys were waiting for me. I would ask what he did all night, and he would remind me that he wasn't the one who wanted to get married and have kids. I stopped asking.

But over the years and with greater responsibilities, I lived for the kids and struggled to tolerate Eric. It often felt like I had to mother him too. The video games and football that consumed his time outside of work as a young man never changed. Funny how resentment can take over the space where love used to be, even without knowing it was in the room. He still expected me to serve him, have dinner on the table every night, do his laundry, and tend to the responsibilities of the home and children.

The more challenges we faced, the more he retreated away from the family. He knew I would handle it, so he let me. I'm no saint, and irritation would bubble up from time to time. I tried many different ways to ask for help and to share that he wasn't a partner or taking on his share of parenting. You never knew exactly when it would hit, but you always knew it would. He would snap in anger; no, that is not the right word, it was rage. I saw this when we first met, but he explained things that happened in his childhood and would apologize later.

Over time, the apologies stopped, but after he raged on me, the kids, and the house, he would leave or get lost in football or video games. When he did resurface, it was like nothing ever happened. I admit I was happy the angry version seemed to be tucked away, but nothing ever changed except my knowing what seemed to trigger him. I felt like a single parent with four children.

I grew to not like him, and I've heard you stop being attracted to someone you have to mother, and I agree with that. I talked of divorce many times, but there were three things that always stopped me. The first was truly believing that divorce was selfish and only solved problems for the adults, creating hardships on the children. The second was that I had nowhere to go and no financial way to leave. The third was the thought of sharing custody. I believed I was protecting the kids when I became his target. There were times he was on the boys, and I was able to direct him onto me instead. I was afraid of his temper enough to not want him alone with the kids.

During fights, I would tell him that as soon as the kids graduated, I was gone. I wasn't going to do to them what my parents did to us. He would smirk at me and say I wasn't going anywhere. This confused me as he didn't seem to like me and didn't want the responsibilities of a family.

Although he would tell me he couldn't control his rage, I noticed it never happened in public or with anyone else. He wasn't just a verbal assailant. His fists and fury would fly. I was hit once. He came at me with his fist to my face, and I flinched. He quickly snapped out of the state he was in and became soft and so apologetic, saying he was trying to scare me but never meant to hit me. He was going to hit the wall next to my face.

The next fight, I just stood still, and he would break everything around me, trying to make me think he would hit me. Holes in doors and walls, broken picture frames, anything he could pick up and throw. Not showing my fear enraged him more.

Then night would come, and he would wake up in a wonderful mood, acting as if nothing had happened, even when he saw me gluing things back together. Sometimes he would even patch the holes he had put in the walls.

I tried to give the kids a good life, but we always struggled financially. I would work up to three jobs at a time, knowing we needed funds but trying desperately to be home when they were. The memories of needing my mom around were very strong and it very much was at the forefront of what drove me. I changed jobs regularly, trying to work around their schedules. Most often, I would work overnights so that the kids were sleeping when I was gone, and I didn't have to with Eric.

As the kids got older in middle and high school, the hours of homework and daily calls of late assignments and tardiness really put so much stress on the home. We all dreaded the time after school activities. It was a constant battle to address the school voicemails and lectures of the importance of their school work. Eric was much more book smart and able to understand the work they were doing, but he had no patience, and fights would ensue if the kids struggled to understand or just didn't care to listen to him.

Eric and I ended up falling into a rhythm where he would only come home right as I needed to leave for my night shift or after the kids were in bed. He brought a cot into his office and would play video games there and who knows what else hours after work was over just to avoid the tedious battle of dinner, chores, and homework.

I got into a rhythm of my own where I would fight the good fight, clean the house, tuck the kids in, lower the lights, light a candle, and softly play the piano. I felt so much peace in the late evenings and cherished that we made it through another night, my babies were sleeping, and calm was felt in the home.

We did this for some time, and it seemed to work well. Eric's rage was much more rare as it was family life that seemed to trigger it. I felt like a single parent, but there was peace in the home. No fighting or yelling when he wasn't around.

I found a wonderful job working in an adoption agency as a counselor that allowed me some flexibility in my schedule. My role was to work with the birth mother and the birth families, providing them with support, resources, and counseling. Helping them decide to parent or choose a family, making sure they could receive prenatal care through to post-counseling after placement and relinquishment. I was present for many of my girls with no support during deliveries and often found myself with custody of the infants while the adoptive parents were either still being chosen or traveling to arrive.

Shoes sat by the bed for the late-night calls and a spare car seat just in case. Although I dreamed of adopting children, this really felt like I found my career purpose. The first Tuesday of each month, I was in court for relinquishment hearings. I felt well-rounded here. Being the accounting manager for the agency, helping so many people, supporting them in very difficult times, providing resources, attending court... I just felt like I had come full circle. I felt so much love and compassion for their journey and the hard decisions in front of them.

I also learned about all the resources available to help people in these situations that I never knew about when I was in this position. There are many programs I could have benefited from, but no one ever told me about them. I thought I had no options and promised to make sure none of my girls felt hopeless.

One late night, I was sitting at the piano, letting my fingers release the tension of the day. The kids were in bed, the house was clean with no trace of the homework battles fought earlier that evening when the doorbell rang. I looked at the clock— it was almost 11:00 p.m.! I was so irritated as Eric disrupted the peace and set the dogs off. He must have forgotten his keys again. I walked to the door and flung it open, returning to the piano. But it wasn't Eric.

Two police officers stepped into the house, and I turned when I heard the static of a walkie. I jumped up and honestly expected to hear that Eric was in an accident.

It was so much worse than that.

TWELVE

They asked if Ren lived here and if he was home. Ren!!??? I said that he was in bed and to please tell me what was going on. They told me that a girl from school had come into the police station with her father a few hours ago, stating that Ren tried to rape her! They were there to talk to Ren and get a statement.

I began to shake visibly, and my mind was just in shock. There is no way this is right. They have to have the wrong boy. I insisted that Ren was at school, then football practice, and then took the bus home, which is where he has been since with me. They asked me to get Ren. I first asked to call Eric and told him to please come home as there were police there for Ren. He said he would come.

I went to Ren's room and gently tried to wake him. I needed to talk to him before telling him why. He would be so scared to hear that police were looking for him. His back was to me, and I gently rubbed his back and told him to please wake up. He rolled over, and I asked him if anything happened at school today, and he just said no.

I let him know what I was told and that he needed to come upstairs to give a statement to the police that were there. He jumped up, and I could tell he was terrified. He kept saying he swore he doesn't know what they are talking about. We walked upstairs together.

Ren has always been polite and respectful, and tonight was no different. He introduced himself, and although he never interrupted, his head was shaking in disbelief. I watched intently and just wanted to protect him, not knowing what to expect next.

The officers explained who reported him. I knew of her as the kids would often walk together from the bus stop to the house, where Ren would come in and she would continue walking. I remember some time ago asking if there was something between them, as she always seemed flirty. He said they were just friends. I knew she lived further down the neighborhood but didn't know where.

The officers were asking pointed questions about why he was on the late bus and why she was, if this was normal, and if he knew why she would claim rape. Ren spoke clearly, but you could hear his voice break occasionally, and he would quickly try to regain his composure. He let them know that he either had football practice or weights every day after school and that he didn't know why she was on the late bus but that she took the same bus every day and they both walked down the same street to get home. He swore that she wasn't his girlfriend and nothing happened that day. They were just friends.

They asked more questions, which he answered, and then stood up to leave just as Eric came in. The officers thanked us for our time and said that they were here only to get a statement and would be in touch if anything else was needed.

Ren was almost in tears once the door shut, and he tried to retreat to his room, but I stopped him. I told him to tell me everything that happened and why she would have come up with this story. I promised him that no matter what he told me, I would always be by his side. He repeated the same information he provided earlier. I asked him point-blank, "Did you try to get physical with her?" His voice was much louder and firm now, and he said no again.

Eric's approach was just accusatory, and he thought he could threaten more out of him. Ren jumped back at him, and they started fighting when I got between them and said this wasn't helping and let Ren leave to his room.

The next morning, we followed the same routine. There was a group that would carpool in the morning, so he didn't take the bus to school, and I told him I would pick him up after. The school called me within the first thirty minutes of classes starting and had other plans. The girl's father was there and really upset that Ren was in class. I was asked to come down.

When I arrived at the school, there were cops, security, the principal, and Ren waiting for me. The school had decided that it would be best for Ren to leave and not return until they could investigate the claim. I was told that the girl and her father were locked in a room until they were assured that Ren was not allowed there anymore. I left with a shaken and embarrassed son.

By the fourth day, cops arrived at the house again late in the morning. We were given a temporary restraining order with a court date to appear later that month. I was told that a parent would need to be with Ren at all times until then. The school was notified and they suspended him, and he was not to be within a certain distance of any school. Now, picking up my younger children became an issue. Eric's company was very lenient, but he never offered to be home to help, and I only asked once. There was some stupid excuse for anything I needed. I preferred being the one with the kids and didn't want to worry about any unnecessary battles with him anyway.

I called the detective often that presented his card at the school for more details. All of my calls went to voicemail to leave my name and number. Eventually, he called back letting me know that the girl claimed this occurred in a stairwell at the school. I was sure there were cameras and asked for any evidence to support her claim. Ren insisted this was not true.

He confirmed that the school did have video footage and it would be released to them. I begged to see this video but was only told that they would let me know. As the court date was getting closer, I kept persisting that we needed this before going before the judge.

I worked on reaching out to attorneys to help us, but the retainers alone were more than we had. As the court date neared, I had learned what this hearing date was about and knew we needed someone to help navigate this unknown world. I leveraged everything we could and had a brief call with an attorney.

I still needed to work and made up a lie about why Ren needed to come with me. I didn't tell a soul about this to protect my son from judgement. Not my family, neighbors, or friends. Ren was miserable and apologetic but stood by his story.

Just four days before the hearing, I was called by the school letting me know they would allow us to watch the school's surveillance video in the company of an officer and the principal. We were not allowed to receive a copy and were told a specific time to come. Directions not to come any earlier as the girl's father would be there able to see it before we did. Ren could come as well. I was happy to see the relief on his face and his eagerness to go. I called the attorney first and then Eric and told him to please come as soon as possible as we weren't given much notice.

Everyone was there waiting in a huddle outside the main doors of the high school to be called in. No one spoke; we just waited. We were met outside and directed into a room off the main office. There was a small tv on a round table that took up most of the room. We huddled close to the screen, and we were told there was no audio. The picture quality was poor. I put my hand on Ren's back, but he pulled away.

The empty stairwell was showing on the screen with a large landing dividing the turn of the stairs. Coming from the top of the stairs, the girl was walking down, and Ren was behind her. Only the backs of them were showing, but the girl would turn and look up toward Ren twice with a smile, and her mouth was moving. I was straining to try and read her lips, but the video was so grainy.

When they got to the landing, she turned around and backed up to the wall as Ren was almost to the landing. She was now facing the camera so we could see her. She was smiling and talking. Ren walked toward her and placed his right arm on the wall next to her. She turned away and walked toward the lower set of stairs. Ren followed behind her, and when they reached the first steps, Ren's hand appeared to hold the rail, which covered our view of her mostly. You could see her hand raise and her headphone being reached for.

That was the end of the video. That was it. I just looked around to see if they were going to pull up another video coming out of the stairwell, but there was nothing. This is where she told the officers the assault took place. We just stood there for what seemed like enough time to feel the silence of disbelief. Everything that had happened to this point centered around this thirty-two-second video? Nothing happened!

I looked to my left and asked the officer and principal if this was all and if so, everything should be dropped, right? Our attorney reached for my arm and said that we would work it out at the set hearing unless the family drops the restraining order before then.

***

Ren, Eric, and I rode to the courthouse together. I begged Eric to let the attorney speak and that any outbursts from us would only hurt us. The attorney was waiting and quickly ushered us into a small room. He was only interested in hearing from Ren, who told him the same thing he told the officers. The attorney then briefed us on what the crowded courtroom would look like, and the judge had a full docket, calling one case up at a time, spending little more than a handful of minutes on each one. He told us not to look at anyone except the judge and especially not the girl and her father, who were already seated.

A few cases were called before us, but we really didn't have to wait long. The clerk next to the judge called our case, and the attorney walked Ren up to his desk. The girl, her father, and their attorney joined them. Ren kept his head forward, but the father didn't look away from Ren. I couldn't see the clerk anymore as they stood in a huddle getting directions. When they came back, our attorney said that they agreed to meet with him privately before the judge called us; to sit tight, and he would return shortly.

We listened as case after case was called and dismissed with seeming coldness as people were leaving as quickly as they were called up. Fates were decided in mere moments.

When our attorney returned, he sat next to Ren and quietly updated us on his meeting. The girl's father shared that he is a single father, and his older daughter had been raped. He taught his daughters to cry 'rape' if they ever felt uncomfortable. He said that he saw the video also and was willing to drop the restraining order!

The intense relief was palpable. We still had to go through with the proceedings, where he would share that they are dropping the charge. When our case was called, her attorney stated that they were dropping the restraining order. Our attorney spoke in agreement, and we were done.

THIRTEEN

Eager to regain some normalcy, I was so grateful for the video and that this was over. As soon as I had the court transcript, I reached out to the school to provide them with a copy and see how we could go forward. The father still requested that Ren not be able to return to the school to make sure there was no retribution on his daughter.

We were sad as Ren had so many friends and was on the football team and in the bachelorette program, which wasn't offered at the other schools nearby. I'm sure he was thinking these things also but just wanted to put this all behind him and didn't want to run into her again either.

I got to work making phone calls to the schools to pull transcripts and to find the funds to pay for the attorney. My goal was to do all of this before Trafton and Jessica came home from school so that home could get back to normal. We were waiting for the final approval to move schools when the doorbell rang. It was two officers.

They were serving us with a restraining order again! I explained that this was a mistake as it was dropped. I was told this one is not from the family but from the state and to contact our attorney for more information. I told myself not to panic as I'm sure this was some clerical error. That the state and the courts must have crossed information. They had more to inform me of though. This restraining order wasn't to keep him from being near her, it was anyone her age and younger!

Like I said, our marriage was to a point where I handled things and tried not to ask anything of him. I knew he would come up with some lame reason he needed to leave when it was clear I needed help. I found that by just letting him go, he was triggered less and there was more peace in our home.

For years I had felt like I had so many balls in the air that if I were to drop anything, there would be no one there to catch them. I always felt overwhelmed and tightly wound which didn't seem fair. I had calendars and spreadsheets to keep tight schedules to just keep my head above water. I wanted to play and be a fun parent but felt the heavy responsibility on me to keep things going.

The attorney had me read the order I was just handed over the phone and said he would call me back. I had plenty to keep me busy but my stomach had this heavy pain. When he called back, he shared that the State of Colorado was the one who filed the restraining order and did so after the court dropped the original one. That they now filed and, in his words, were going to make an example out of Ren. I just didn't understand. With the video and any lack of truth to her story, how do they have the right!? He said we need to save it for the new hearing that was scheduled in three weeks.

I decided to tell Ren now as I had held off until I got some answers. Ren just looked down and didn't say anything. He didn't have to as I tried to fill the empty space with all the information I obtained and the assurance that I would fight for him and stand by his side. Ren was never the cuddly or affectionate kind and he kept his feelings close. I waited for a bit after hugging him with no return and left him alone in his room.

When Eric came home that night, many hours after work was over, I told him as well. The next afternoon, there was a knock at the door. I'm scared of that door now and didn't think it could get worse, but there stood a woman handing me a card, stepping into the doorway to speak with Ren and his parents. She was from Child Protective Services.

She prodded into details about who lived in the home, with names and ages. She then laid a copy of the restraining order on the table in front of us and pointed to the language of anyone her age and younger, and proceeded to tell me that included his siblings. I begged her for help. I tried to explain that this was all a mistake and I had no way to separate the children. She outlined conditions that we would have to maintain until the court date, that I immediately agreed to before understanding them fully.

We had to get alarms on Ren's bedroom windows, door, and bathroom. If he wasn't in the immediate presence of either myself or Eric, he had to be in his room or bathroom with the alarms set to indicate if he was to open the door. With Trafton and Jessica in school, he had more freedom, but while they were there, he was stuck by my side or locked in his room, which he preferred. When he went to sleep, his alarms were set. Ren looked defeated and really withdrew into himself.

Two days later, when the kids came home from school, they told me they were pulled into the principal's office, and this same social worker was asking some pretty uncomfortable questions at the elementary school. I was so angry and called, leaving a message for her, but it was not returned.

Weeks later, we were in court again. Instead of the temporary restraining order being dropped, it was no longer temporary, and the District Attorney's office was now taking over the case.

There are so many details of what all came next, and I wish I didn't remember every single one, but the facts were that the state has very strict laws to protect against assault, to include perceived assault, and Ren made her think he could have raped her, so they were going to charge him as a sex offender. The DA was giving us two options. The first was that Ren would be arrested and have his day in court being held in juvenile detention until then, which could be upwards of a year. The State was going to charge him as an adult regardless of his actual age. If we lost, he would be a registered sex offender for his entire life.

The second option was a very expensive program governed by the DA's office that would include mandatory juvenile sex offender therapy, random lie detector screening, periodic substance testing, and other strict requirements. A book really of rules. That a certified adult was required to be in his presence at all times. He could start at the new school, but a certified adult had to walk him in and sign him over to a designated school representative who also had to stay with him. He would lose all freedom, but if he completed their program, he would be released from the restrictions and could resume a normal life. He would stay on probation until he was 18, but with no issues, his record would be expunged.

This program had their own psychologists, locations, guardians, and child protective service persons they chose. The DA made it very clear that if we didn't pay on time, if we didn't immediately respond to any and all orders for polygraphs and testing with cash only, if we missed any therapy sessions, also paid in cash, Ren would be kicked out and back to the first option.

He told us that most families opt for the second option but due to the high costs, turn their children over to the state, and the state will then pick up the costs. The length of the program was around two years but depended on their therapists' assessment and could last for many years past that.

So from what I am hearing, we either turn him over to be held in juvi and hope for the best in court whenever that would be, relinquish my son to the state, or figure out how to pay their fees. We didn't have much and didn't have any family support, but I just had to make this work! I looked at Ren and said I would figure it out and put us in the program.

The certification cost was $600.00 per adult, so Eric decided that I should be the only one to take it to save us $600.00. I resented him for this as I couldn't do everything alone and needed to keep my job. I protested, but a fight began, and I just left the room. There was no reasoning with him, and I didn't need a new fight on my hands. We refinanced the house to pull everything out that we could.

Somehow I managed the appointments, kids, and work but next to no sleep. I was so determined to save my son from this absolute unfair example they were making out of him, making sure not to do a thing to risk being removed from the program.

I don't know how far into it we were, but Social Services and the assigned guardian ad litem came to let us know that we could no longer allow Ren to be in the same home as Trafton and Jessica. That by doing so violated the restraining order, and we would be kicked out of the program. I pleaded for any leniency, but there was none to be given. Either Ren has to leave the home or Trafton and Jessica do. Defeated but not giving up, I said I would leave with

Ren to a hotel until we could figure something out. As I was the only certified parent, it could only be me.

I called Eric and told him the news and asked him to please go through the certification so we could take turns. I didn't want to leave my babies. He said he would but never got around to it. Ren and I had a scheduled meeting with the DA. I requested that we be allowed to continue with the alarms and let Ren stay home. That separating the kids was impossible. We had to sleep in the car at times as we couldn't afford the costs. I explained how we had been managing with the alarms and begged for this to continue. I was told no.

I looked at apartments, trying to find something to hold us over. As I was the one renting, it was only my income they would look at, and with my very part-time hours now to manage our new schedules, I didn't make enough with the mortgage also. I shared what we were going through and asked if there were any programs to help us pay the exorbitant fees. He shared that there were no exceptions to this option.

Ren said to do it. To sign him over to the state. I didn't even look away from the road but swore I would never give him up. Social services made regular visits, and I begged for help. She shared there were foster homes that housed juveniles with the same offenses but without the state's custody; we would be responsible for the cost, which neared $4000.00 per month. She even suggested that it is easier to find a place for the younger kids as their foster costs wouldn't be as high because of the specialty home Ren would have to be in. Hell no!

Ren and I kept hopping from place to place but knew I couldn't continue the length of the program and not being able to see my other children. Running out of options, I called to set a time to discuss placing Ren in one of their homes, insisting that I am able to continue the transportation to and from school and see him every day. And as soon as I could figure an-other way, I would pull him out. They agreed.

The homes for these boys were full, but they were anticipating some changes soon. In the mean-time, he was able to go to a facility that included round-the-clock professionals in a facility that, al-though locked, had a school, inner courtyard, and programs for the kids there. I swore to Ren that this would be temporary, and with his schedule, he would only be there overnight, really. I signed some papers with them and really had good feelings about this place and the many staff members I met.

There was a lot of staff on at all times. All licensed professionals who seemed to get along well and cared for the kids living there.

FOURTEEN

I was up each morning at 4:00 a.m. to shower and make breakfast for the family. I packed up food for Ren and drove the forty-five minutes from the house to the facility. I met him in a receiving room, and we had breakfast in the car. I drove him to school, signing him over at the office. From there, I went back home and got to take the littles to school. Then, I was off to work. I had to figure out how to pick up Ren, take him to therapy, and back to the facility and not neglect the kids. Without telling anyone why, I had a neighbor let the kids stay for a bit after school until Eric would get home. We are now many months after this all started.

I was really impressed with this facility. Ren liked it too, and the staff was just amazing. This also gave me the ability to be home with Trafton and Jessica. I asked our social worker if he could stay there through the program. Ren was doing really well under the circumstances, and we were managing the schedule well enough. Even the staff wrote letters to keep him there. But no, was the answer. Because of the sex offender charge, this was only a temporary option until they could place him in a home specific to his offense. I just kept hoping they wouldn't find another place.

Several weeks went by, and I was at home after dropping Ren off and playing with the kids when the doorbell rang. I got up to answer it and again was met by a pair of officers. They asked if Ren was home, and I told them no, confused as to why they were there but also how they didn't know he was in the facility. Initially, I thought they were doing a check to make sure he was not there, but they explained they had orders to bring him into the juvenile detention center because he failed a polygraph. They couldn't answer any of the other questions I shot at them and could only say that once booked, the judge would see him in court the following day to hear of the charges.

I was sick. Everything we were doing was to keep him out of juvi, and I really felt scared for him. I gave them the address of the facility, and they called dispatch for direction. I asked if I could follow them to be there and talk to Ren first. They were told that the address was out of their jurisdiction, so they would arrange for other officers to pick him up. It was too late tonight, so they would pick him up tomorrow.

My head was spinning, and I had to force myself to focus. It was Thursday. If the other officers were going to book him tomorrow, he would be stuck there until Monday before seeing the judge! I told them my thoughts and asked if I brought him in myself tonight, would the judge see him tomorrow? They confirmed that once booked, the following business day would be the court hearing. So that was the plan. There was no other way. I was told that I had to have him there by 10:00 p.m. so he would be on the docket for Friday. The officers contacted the facility to let them know to expect me.

Eric wasn't home, so I called desperately, trying to reach him to be with the kids. I planned how I'd stay calm and how I would break the news to Ren. If Eric hurried, I could grab some food with Ren before the curfew set and have a chance to tell him that I would be there with our attorney and to ask what he may have lied about.

I broke down and cried, begging for God to help me, just imagining how scared Ren would be and how helpless I was to fix this. I couldn't understand how the state could do this with proof that nothing ever happened. I was sick at the thought of being the one who turned him in and leaving him there. It was all I knew to do, and I was the only one who could do it.

I couldn't wait any longer and asked my neighbor if they would keep an eye on the kids until Eric made it home. I kissed the kids goodnight and ran out the door. Unable to see the road through my tears, I just needed to get it together. Running off the road or showing up with red, puffy eyes was not going to give any comfort to Ren. I got there and could see the confusion on his face. He didn't know why I was checking him out and could tell something was wrong. I told him that I would explain everything in the car.

Ren didn't want to eat anything. He was shaking but trying to hide it and was looking out his window, but I could see his reflection as tears streamed down his face while I stumbled through my reasoning to turn him in now. Ren said he had no idea what he would have lied about.

I decided to lie myself and told him that I was actually told what he lied about. Hoping this would convince him to open up so we could prepare a defense, Ren managed to tell me that they asked if he had ever been inappropriate before. He answered no but told me that he made inappropriate advances on another girl when he was ten. I didn't respond. I didn't know how to or what this all meant.

We drove the rest of the way in silence. I couldn't believe what I was doing. We walked up together into the building and to the bullet-proof window. My legs were trying to buckle beneath me for betraying my son. I had to sign documents that I was turning him in. I tried to hug him, but he turned away, and I just said I was so sorry and I would be there in the morning. I stood frozen as they ushered him behind the bars, which led to a heavy door closing behind them.

***

I didn't sleep at all, thinking of how scared he must be. Trying to have a nice morning with the kids, I made sure to be present with them before dropping them off at school. I called the attorney but was told he would try to make it as he would be in the courthouse adjacent to another case. I drove straight to the courthouse. I asked where to go and was told that I needed to watch for them to post the docket outside of a particular room. I sat and watched, imagining what was happening to Ren. When they pinned the papers to the wall, I ran up looking for his name and our time. I called to let Eric know, and he met me there.

    When the doors opened, a large group had now gathered, and we streamed in, filling every seat in the large courtroom. I tried to save a seat for the attorney, but there were too many people. My eyes were darting from the door I came in from and the doors at the front of the room. We were given instructions on the behaviors expected. It felt like forever when the door to the right of the judges' bench opened.

    Officers walked in first and scanned the room. Behind them came some boys dressed in bright orange jumpsuits with their hands and feet shackled and chained to each other. They filed in, and I was sick, not ever thinking this could be happening to Ren. Then I saw him. He was not looking up, only down at his shoes. I was sick seeing him cuffed like he was dangerous. Hearing the chains hit the floor. My heart dropped so hard I could feel it. The boys were ordered to sit, and two other officers filed in behind them.

I tried to make eye contact to let him know I was here and to see that he was okay, but he never looked anywhere but in front of him or at the officers barking orders at them.

When I heard them call a case number and then our last name, I panicked. Still no sign of the attorney. They brought Ren down to the defense table with an officer right at his side, and Eric and I were allowed to sit at the table just in front of him. He still wouldn't make any eye contact with me. The judge stated the case of the State of Colorado against Ren and gave a court date. The officer then stood Ren up and returned him to the witness stand where all the boys were. What? He can't stay locked up! All of this was just to set a different date??

I sat back down in the crowd, trying to stay as close to Ren as I could. I didn't know what the court date was for or what was happening next, but I stayed there until they walked all the boys out the same door they came in. Tears filled my eyes in disbelief and utter confusion.

I asked the clerk outside the room where I should go next and was told to come back on the court date. That was almost a week away!! They couldn't keep Ren. I needed to take him away from this place. Why was he shackled? He wasn't dangerous. I waited in lines, taking numbers and waiting to ask for help, but no one would help me or give me any information.

The drive home was agonizing, with the most horrible thoughts racing. Was he kicked out of the program? When could I see him? Is he okay? I was terrified for him.

The attorney called later and apologized for not making it there and asked what happened. He said that this was just procedure, and we needed to talk with the therapist and DA to prepare for the court date. He gave me the number to the juvenile detention center to set up visitation. I probably left eight messages within a few minutes when someone finally answered. The soonest I could go in was the next afternoon.

It was winter, and snow covered the ground. It was bitter cold as the temperature was in the negatives with the wind. I was given a list of rules about my visit and made sure I followed them all to not risk this time with him. I walked in and made it through security and an ID check. Being led into a large waiting room with only a woman and a teenage girl sitting against the wall.

Behind me, I saw the same orange jumpsuits through a window in an outdoor courtyard. I walked closer, seeing about twenty boys who all looked the same, scanning them for my son. They were shivering and just walking around the small space.

When I found Ren, I was shocked to see that he had no coat or shoes! When I checked him in, he had both. I scanned the other boys, trying to make sense of why some had coats and shoes and others didn't. I couldn't break myself from the window in hopes that Ren seeing me here would comfort him. He never looked up.

When the boys were led inside through a door away from me, I turned to see where I should go. I saw some glass windows at the other side of the room but didn't see anyone there, so I just stood there waiting. Finally, a woman walked over and sat in a chair that was much lower than the window and asked who I was here to see and if I had an appointment. She pushed through some papers to sign through a little crack in the glass. I returned them with my ID and was told to have a seat.

FIFTEEN

I waited and waited and waited. It was now well past the appointment time, and I started to worry that they weren't going to bring him out. Finally, they called my name and directed me to a door which opened into a small room with a couple of seats and a small table with a dim lamp lit. There was a door opposite the one I came in and was told to wait.

When the other door opened, Ren came in. Still without shoes. I hugged him but didn't get anything back but a nod. The guard who let him in told us what time we had before he returned, and I asked him about the shoes and coat. He said that the ones he came in with had colors that were associated with gangs, so they were taken. I begged to be able to bring him something different and was told that nothing could be brought in.

I tried to get Ren to talk to me, but he wasn't. I would ask questions, and he would nod yes or no and sometimes would answer briefly. In my nervousness, I just told him all the things I heard from the attorney and about how I would be meeting with the DA and the therapist to be ready for the court date. I probably asked a hundred times if he was okay, if he felt safe, and what it was like. He mumbled that he was fine, but I just didn't believe it. He told me a little about the cells they were in and how he had to be let out to use the bathroom. Other questions were responded with "you don't want to know".

I tried to touch him and comfort him but just wanted him to have some time away from whatever was on the other side of that door. There was silence at the end. When the door opened, I held him so tight as he moved away and through the door.

Every day they let me come, and for as long as they would allow, I was there. Giving him as much information as I had been gathering and about the attorney's confidence that he would be out soon. In the silence which we always had if I stopped talking, without looking at me, Ren told me that the guards called him the pretty boy and would tease the boys. That he asked to be let out to go to the bathroom, and they let another boy who was not quiet about being gay into the bathroom with him and locked them in, taunting and teasing them.

I saw tears fall that he didn't wipe away and asked if anything had happened. He didn't answer. I wanted to tear this building down and raced home to call the attorney, telling him what had happened and asking what he could do. He said anything we did at this point would make it worse for Ren and to focus on the upcoming court date.

I pleaded with God and cursed Him at times for not getting him out of this. I begged for help getting him back in the program so he could come home, wherever that was. At least away from this place.

The court date was finally here. Our attorney was prepared to tell the judge why Ren should be able to continue with the program. That what had happened, when he was ten, was under the age of any legal right to hold him for that. I was always prepared to speak if given the chance.

This time the court only had three cases, three boys in their jumpsuits. At the table next to us was a representative from the DA's office, the guardian ad litem, the social worker, and the therapist who Ren had been ordered to attend her group meetings as part of the program.

The attorney, myself, and Eric were at the defense table, and they shuffled Ren behind us again. I tried to look back, but Ren would look away. I will never forgive them for the shackles.

They presented their case that Ren broke the contract of the program. Our attorney pushed back. Eric and I weren't even looked at by the judge or given any chance to speak. I couldn't believe this was all that was allowed before the judge spoke. He just said that with the evidence presented and the family supporting Ren in the program and meeting all of the requirements, he would release Ren back to the custody of his mother to continue with the program. I heard a breath released from Ren behind me.

The guard ushered him out the back door, and I held my breath, afraid to speak but watching the attorney thank the judge and gather his papers. Why did they take him? What do we do now? Is he going to come home?

Eric left, and I went to the juvenile center to wait. I was given a bag of his belongings, including his coat and shoes. Ren came out in his street clothes, and we moved through the parking lot to the car so quickly. I had offered him his shoes, but he didn't slow down. It felt like we were holding our breath until we drove out of the parking lot.

I drove in the opposite direction of the courthouse just to create some distance, but I didn't know where to go. We can't go home. Do we return to the facility? Do we have to go now? Ren was silent, and I knew he would talk if he wanted to, but I'm sure he was wondering what was next for him too. I pulled through a drive-through and ordered food and a drink. I didn't think he would eat, but I drove to a nearby empty park and told him I needed to make some calls. He grabbed the bag and walked to a tree and just sat down facing away from me.

Apparently, Ren had to be discharged from the facility, and social services said he could not go back there. We were reminded not to violate the restraining order, or he would be arrested. They were working on placing him in a foster home for sex offender boys in the DA program, but until then, we had to figure something out.

I was so angry with the state but made sure to just be agreeable and not show my feelings. If we had a chance for a court hearing today, I would take it. We had no control; we didn't get to pick our therapist; they did. We didn't have any ability to question them. If we wanted the court hearing, he would be held in juvi until then, and the docket was out for many months. There was no way I was going to send him back there.

Over a month had passed, and the call came that a home was found. I insisted, as always, that this was a voluntary placement where I would continue to take him to school and visit every day. They said there would be no change to our arrangement.

The day came to meet the foster mother at the social services office and to turn Ren over to her care. The agony of every move tore me apart, but I knew we just had to get through to the end of this program. Ren was really distant and did exactly what was asked of him, but you could see his spirit was broken. I kept repeating that this would be over soon. I didn't believe that, and neither did he.

Eric met us there a few minutes before our 3:30 p.m. appointment that Friday. We were taken to the third floor to a large conference room with a long desk and chairs that could seat thirty people with a full wall of windows at the other end. Our social worker, guardian ad litem, and a weathered woman were already sitting with a security guard standing just outside the door. Introductions were made, and we sat down opposite everyone else at this oversized table. In my head, I was expecting a kind, soft woman as the foster mom, but she was unwashed, wearing a ratty tank top and shorts with two-inch fake nails, missing teeth, and not very friendly.

The social worker started talking about Ren and why he was here and the charges against him. They spoke about where he was before being taken into the detention center. The details of the restraining order and nothing else. Then they asked the foster mom what questions she had for us.

She started by sharing how many boys like Ren she had taken in and how many years she had been at it. A long list of her rules was tapped out with her fingernails clanking on the desk. She was gruff and warden-like. I felt sick to my stomach thinking of Ren leaving with her but listened, waiting for my chance to ask her questions. Her stare bore into Ren directly, never looking away.

As she was going through her rules, she said that until Ren earned her trust, there would be no phone calls allowed and no leaving the house for at least the first month. I tried to hold my objections for her to be done, but this was too much for me, and I jumped in.

Looking at the social worker, I shook my head no. I explained how things would be, that this was already agreed on, and that there would be contact with me anytime he needed it, and I would be taking him out for school every day, that there was more abuse in foster homes, and I was not going to let this happen.

So much for being calm.

SIXTEEN

This woman started shouting at me! The social worker spoke over us all, and the guard was now standing in the doorway. We settled down, and the social worker was now explaining how things had been with Ren's schedule. The foster mom stood up and defiantly opposed repeating her rules and that there would be no such interference by 'his mother'. None of the boys had family involvement, and Ren would not be getting special treatment. My response was that this meeting was over then, and we would find something else. I stood up to leave.

The social worker stood up also and let me know I don't have a choice. I was on fire and shot back that this was a voluntary placement and there was no way I would leave my son with her! The woman started shouting that she wouldn't take him anyway with a crazy mother and no wonder why he is in trouble and other nasty comments. I wanted to reach across the table and tear her apart.

The guard was now at the table and demanded we sit down. The social worker gathered the papers in front of her and said flatly to me, "It is no longer voluntary, and they would be taking Ren now.'"

She gave a nod to the guard, who started making his way toward us. I jumped up and stood in front of the chair Ren was sitting on and said, "I will jump out of this window with him before I ever allow them to take Ren." The guard moved quickly toward me, and I threatened him not to come any closer.

For the first time, Ren spoke in a quiet and broken voice, saying, "Just let them take me." Eric agreed and told me, "Let him go." I looked incredulously at Eric with so much disdain and repeated that I was the only one who would fight for Ren, and he is not going anywhere. The guard was now right on me, and I was being told that if I didn't move aside for them to take Ren, I would be arrested. I shouted for him to arrest us both, that the jail would be safer than with that woman!

I looked at the glass wall and the chair next to it and tried to plan how I'd break the glass and force Ren to jump out with me. I pushed Ren behind my back and slowly backed us up to the glass side of the room. I knew I looked hysterical, so I calmed my voice, which became deep and deliberate, and I told them that there are no reasons that we can't continue to keep him with me. This was to be a voluntary placement to help us, and we don't want this anymore. I will not allow them to take Ren.

The guard and guardian ad litem were now within reach of me, but I wouldn't let them get to Ren. Eric was standing near the door. Coward. The foster mom was arguing with the social worker, saying they couldn't pay her enough to deal with me. As the guard reached around to grab cuffs, I told them that I wanted to speak with the DA or a judge, that they had no right to change the conditions we had in place. That everyone in this room was supposed to be here to protect Ren, and no one was! The guard told Ren to come to him, and Ren tried to move past me, but I pushed back to the wall, trying to pin him, and reaching back with my arms to stop him.

A second guard was called and took over. He said that I just needed to comply and could talk to the judge on Monday to get him back. I laughed and said that I knew better than that. Getting a child out of foster care would be harder than that, and that I should be able to leave, and they can talk to the judge on Monday.

I told him that they were all putting my son in harm's way, that we had done nothing but comply, and that my son would stay with me, which is in compliance with the court. That they tricked me and lied that this was a voluntary placement and they were reneging on it. This went on for a while, and it was getting dark outside the window. They were not relenting, and I was never going to.

They kept telling me that I had to turn him over, and we weren't getting any closer to me winning this terrifying battle. Even Eric and Ren weren't supporting me. The social worker was telling someone on the phone that this was to be a voluntary placement, but the judge said it is no longer voluntary. I told the guard to let me talk to the judge. They pushed back, saying the courts are now closed, and judges don't call people on the phone. I pushed again, saying that I would see them then on Monday with Ren. They would not take him, period.

Why were they doing this? Why did they seem so intent on taking my son? There has to be more to this than I just don't understand.

The social worker spoke, saying that they were closed now and everyone needed to go home, and I was making this harder on everyone. I agreed and said we were happy to leave, but she only wanted me to give into this placement. Getting that I wouldn't relent, they said to sit down, and they would see what could be done. The foster mom left the room, and so did the guardian ad litem.

The social worker was trying to tell me that it was going to be okay, but I pushed back on her, saying I don't trust her. She knew what I expected and promised me that this was voluntary, and Ren's schedule wouldn't change. It was her job to protect Ren, and she only cared about quitting time so she could go home to her family while tearing mine apart.

The first guard came to the doorway and said that he had a judge on the phone who was willing to talk with me. I would have to leave Ren to go to the foyer for the call. I was scanning the room, working out if they could take Ren while I stepped out, expecting they were tricking me. Pushing back, they managed to connect the call to a phone just outside the door. I agreed and moved my chair in the doorway, pulling the cord of the receiver as far as I could to make sure they didn't try leaving with Ren.

It really was a judge on the line. He was very irritated, saying that he understands I am holding many people up who are trying to do their job. I pushed back firmly and clearly. I explained everything I could squeeze into the breath I had, as to not give him a break to interrupt. I told him exactly what we had been doing and that continuing to do so followed the DA program and the restraining order. He was silent for a moment and then agreed! I stood and said "GOOD, now tell them!" and I lifted the phone to the guard near me. Within ten minutes, we were dismissed. My adrenaline didn't come down for days. I was ready to fight.

A new social worker was being assigned as ours now refused, and we continued with our schedule. At night and on the weekends, Ren and I found places to stay or slept in the car. For a brief time, we would go to his grandmother's house an hour south. Ren never complained or asked what was next. He only said I should have let him go. I missed his laugh and the way his face would shine when he was happy. I prayed that we could just get through this and could start healing.

Eric said he wasn't able to manage the children's schedules without me. I didn't believe him, as his boss was a friend of my family's and was always saying he could take whatever time was needed. He clearly wasn't helping me through this, so I called my sister Olivia who lived a few states over. I knew she was home with her young kids while her husband was deployed overseas.

Telling her only that Ren was in some trouble and I just needed help with Trafton and Jessica. I managed to borrow a van that she could use, and she agreed to bring her kids out, treating it like a little vacation. There was plenty of room in the house, and I was so grateful to her. I only got to see her briefly when Ren was in school and I was heading to work.

The social worker needed to meet up for a check-in and wanted Ren and me to come to their office, but I refused. I told her that I would never go there again, but we could meet at Ren's school, a park, or when I found a place for the night, I would give her an address, and we could meet there.

When we met, it was all business. I was told that either I placed Ren or they would place Trafton and Jessica. They found a new home, and she had a court order outlining that it was still voluntary. He would be integrated into the home, which meant Ren would go to the same therapist and school as all the boys in this home. Although I wouldn't be picking him up or dropping him off, they would allow daily visits, and Ren could call anytime he needed.

I could meet the couple first. She told me the price that we would have to pay each month due on the first with no exception. I didn't know how long we could do this as we were running out of the equity we pulled but agreed quickly. I was given a copy of the judge's order and felt confident that I could use this if anyone tried to change one single thing.

I went to the foster home the next day while Ren was at school. It was far north-east and took about an hour to get there. This place was out in the country with nothing nearby but I-70. The social worker told me about the couple and that they had been doing this for some time. They started with young children, but their health wasn't great even though they were young in the beginning. With courses they completed, they moved up to the more challenging kids, and when they took on the juvenile sex offenders, they were able to remodel their home to accommodate the boys.

Neither of them works outside the home. She told me that it cost the state thousands per boy per month to pay this couple for their specialty. They could only have five boys and just had an opening. They are one of the prime foster homes that get to choose who they admit. After hearing about Ren and his good behavior, they said they would take him.

We rang the door, and a pleasant woman met us. She was warm and smiling with a hug for the social worker. Her husband came around the corner, and I met him also. They were much older than me, and I scanned them and their home quickly. I was happy to be here and get to know where Ren would be. They were kind and said they understood my concerns but also explained that all the other boys were wards of the state, so Ren was the only one who would have visitors.

She explained that the boys lived downstairs, and they lived upstairs. There were cameras and locks everywhere that would alert them and the police if any were tripped. She pointed out the large van in front and shared that she drives the boys to school and therapy and brings them home together. She said Ren would join them, and it was important to her that they all moved together so she could manage them best.

I noted that the home was meager, but the massive tv and electronics around it seemed out of place. She shared, mostly to the social worker, that they had some friends over and would buzz the boys to come clean up when they were done. I didn't like hearing that, but I needed to choose my battles, and this wasn't it.

She got up and told me to follow her. With the boys in school, I could see where they lived. We walked down a long flight of stairs into the basement. It was ground level, so there was a lot of light and windows, which was nice. We walked through a big family room area with couches, books, and games. She pointed to one side and shared there were a couple of bedrooms over there while we walked to the opposite side where Ren would be. He would be sharing a room with another boy, and I could see cameras everywhere, including the bedroom and bathroom. I asked about that, and she said it was pointed away from the actual shower and toilet but that they were required to monitor all spaces.

This was so sad to think of these boys here, but I was so grateful for this option. She let me talk about my need to see him and talk with him to make sure he was okay. They were receptive to my requests, and I proceeded to sign their paperwork. Ren was to come there right after school today.

SEVENTEEN

Olivia was planning to stay for a month, but her husband was being released early, and she was leaving in two days. I was sad for me but happy for her. I appreciated the week-long help she was able to provide for the kids. With this new home for Ren, I thought I could manage it better.

Ren was quiet and looking at his shoes when we drove away from the school. He had to switch schools again and would now be living with a bunch of boys he didn't know. Even his group therapy was changing. I was the only constant in his changing world. That didn't seem to comfort him. I explained the surveillance and described the home, letting him know that I could visit and he could call. I handed him the court order in hopes that would make him feel better.

I took his schoolbooks so I could return them and helped sort out some clothes from the truck that he would need. Ren never cried or showed much emotion, but I could sense his fears. I tried to get him to talk to me, but he just looked out the window.

During my visits, I would ask Ren about the other boys and school, but I only got 'it's fine' in return to every question. The couple was happy with Ren and shared that he was very polite and easy.

Not having to find a place to sleep every night was a relief, but selfishly, my heart felt better when he was near me. I got into a new routine with the kids again and loved that part. I went to sign them up at the rec center for sports and ended up becoming the coach for Jessica's softball team as there weren't enough coaches, and she wouldn't have been able to play. Being her coach also allowed me to schedule when and where practices were held, so I made sure it was at the same park as Trafton's team and just after so I could be there for both of them. We became the DirtDivas.

Things seemed to be moving forward, and I was counting down the new timeline expected by the DA for the program course. Money was always the topic of concern. Since I was able to be with the kids more, Eric was home less. We really didn't see much of each other, and when we did, I was just updating him on my visits with Ren.

I wasn't present anymore when the social worker made visits, but we had pretty regular check-in calls. I was always told that Ren is doing well; the couple only had good things to report about him, but the concern was that he was not integrating as much as they would like. I asked about this. Not integrating in the program or school, causing problems? She hurried to say no; he was always respectful and appropriate and did everything expected of him. They didn't like that Ren was treated special, and it wasn't fair to the other boys that Ren would have visitors but they didn't.

I replied that I'm sorry for those boys and wish they also would have visitors but we knew this from the start. The following week, another check-in call came. Same information as every time, and of course, I am happy to hear that there are no issues with Ren.

Thinking the call was over, she asked me if we were alone or if my kids were with me. I excused myself to go to my bedroom. When I got there, she shared that she and the guardian ad litem met this time with the couple and Ren and have decided that there should be no more visits or calls so that he can better integrate with the boys.

Of course, I said no and referenced the court agreement. She then said that because they all agreed that it would be in Ren's best interest and that my involvement creates unnecessary additional work for all three of them, they were filing the petition to change that order with the court to make it official and to have the judge turn custody over to the state. I protested loudly, and she said that she didn't think I was hurting his progress, but the guardian ad litem did, and she has to work with him long after my case is done, so she must go along with it.

I was fuming now, and in my fear of defeat, I told her that I was recording this call and would see her in court. She immediately disconnected.

I called the guardian ad litem, and when I got his voicemail, I let him have it. I yelled down to the kids to get out to the car while I grabbed my shoes. Running out, I called Eric to tell him what had just happened but only got his voicemail. I then called the foster home and was told they were no longer to take my calls.

We drove to the electronics store to get a recording device so I could actually record these calls. When I got home, I called the attorney and left a message for him as well. The DA's office was next, and getting tired of not reaching anyone, I had the poor kids come with me to the courthouse as the DA's office was connected to their building. I needed to talk to someone who could help me.

A woman was willing to sit with me while I told her what was happening. She said she would get this message to the right people, and someone would call me. I just kept saying they can't do this over and over.

There were no more calls from anyone but my attorney. He learned that they did, in fact, petition the court to take custody of Ren, and a court date was set weeks out. This petition stopped me from visits and calls until it went before the judge. The only thing I could do now was wait.

***

Eric and I drove to court to meet the attorney for a briefing before the hearing. I was happy to be able to see Ren again and wondered who else would be there. All our other experiences were that each side's attorney could talk, and then the judge ruled, and that was the end.

As we sat in the courtroom, there were so many people that filed in around the plaintiff table. So much so that people were standing. The previous social worker, the new social worker, the guards from that night, the foster mom, the guardian ad litem, and the assistant to the DA I had spoken with and his old therapist. At our table was just me, Eric, and the attorney.

My heart just sank. They were all permitted to talk, one by one, telling the judge why they believed Ren was better without his family involved. I was blasted, saying I needed to control everything and was argumentative. The therapist said that she believed I only hurt Ren as I was a teen mom, and my religion was such that he had no outlet. They were all but directly saying it was my fault he was in trouble. They were nasty, and I hated each one. It was unbelievable that they were doing this to make their jobs easier, but not one of them actually cared about Ren.

I have spent so much time trying to understand the motive for all the things that had been happening. Why would they do what they are doing? None of it made any sense. All that was clear was we had no say, and our only option was to go along.

Being a ward of the state was the absolute worst thing for him, and I couldn't believe they were saying these things. Surely the judge would take their 'professional' assessment as truth. There was nothing I could do now. Just listening made me sick. I scribbled a note for the attorney and pushed it to him. It said, "Don't let them take my boy."

After an agonizing, long time to get through each person slamming us as parents and stating their request that the state take custody, it was our turn. The judge only spoke with our attorney as always, and I couldn't believe any chance was now in the hands of someone we had to pay to be there.

Our attorney stood and spoke to the judge, saying all the things we rehearsed with the request to keep the course we have been on. It took under two minutes for him to finish. My heart sank. I knew we just lost him. This was the first time I truly felt defeated.

The judge then spoke, thanking everyone for their time and professionalism, and started to summarize the case before him to the clerk. Then, for the first time in all the court hearings, he looked at Eric and asked if he had anything he wanted to add. Hope filled my heart as it leaped up behind my eyes, pushing out tears.

Eric was on my left side, and Ren was to my right. I looked at Eric as he started to stand, never letting go of the armrests, and said, "No, your honor," and sat down.

I looked at him in disbelief, and at that very moment, I hated him and would never forgive him. Any love or any respect I had for him was gone in that instant. He didn't look at either myself or Ren, and I was so disgusted and couldn't believe my ears.

I looked up at the judge, and he said to me, "Do you have anything you want to add before I make the judgement?" I stood up so quickly that if you told me my feet left the ground, I wouldn't doubt it. I hadn't prepared anything, as we never got to speak, but I was ready for this moment.

I looked right at the judge, knowing that I had nothing left to lose, and said, "How dare you take my son from me! The ONLY person in this room that cares about this boy is ME!!". Pointing in the direction of the other table but not breaking eye contact, I continued, "Not one person over there cares for my son and is only here to make their jobs easier. We have done everything that was asked of us. We have paid the fees and followed the rules and danced when they said dance. This all started from a girl that claimed rape. Video proof shows she lied. Maybe she did feel uncomfortable, but he has paid a heavy price. Her family dropped the charges, and the state decided to make an example of him. Ren has been nothing but obedient. If you take him away from me and put him into the horribly broken system, I hope you are not able to sleep at night knowing that you, your decision, has placed him at great risk and punished him unfairly for something he didn't even do. Maybe I was a teen mom, but there hasn't been a day where I didn't put his needs before mine. He has a family. Siblings that love and miss him and a home that needs him back. He is MY boy, and I cannot believe that we are here today talking about taking him away to be thrown in the vat of a terribly broken system. You hold the entirety of his future in your hands."

I sat down and let the tears finally free. The courtroom was silent except for my tears and racing heartbeat. The judge took a moment, then spoke, saying that he was ready to give his judgment.

He said a few things to Ren about keeping up his good behavior and the seriousness of consent. Ren said, "Yes, your Honor" after each sentence. Then he said, "You are discharged to your mother. Go home with your family; this is over. The charges are dismissed."

My gasp of released pain for these years was louder than the uproar of chatter from the other side. I grabbed Ren in my arms so tightly. He didn't hug me back, but that was normal, and I knew he had to be in shock. Not only did the judge deny their requests to gain custody, but the entire claim was dropped! Going from losing my son to it all coming to an end was unbelievable. I kept thanking the judge and God while rushing us out of the courtroom to make sure nothing else was said to change this miracle.

EIGHTEEN

I wouldn't look at or speak with Eric. The drive home was silent. Ren went straight to his room and stayed there the remainder of the day. I picked up the kids and told them it was over.

That night, I told Eric I wanted out. I didn't like him, love him, or respect him, and I was done. After ignoring me for hours, we got into another fight, which ended like all my threats. I had nowhere to go, and we were in deep debt now and just couldn't afford to divorce. I hated this place we were in, and it only got worse the longer we were together.

I came up with a plan that we would live as divorced as possible but live in the same home since I couldn't think of another way. I asked him to sleep on the couch, and he would for a little while and then would always come back up. He would force himself on me in the middle of the night. Every night. I didn't want him to touch me, and that didn't even matter to him. Not knowing what to do, I switched jobs again to work overnights. I was so relieved to not be home at night, and when I did sleep during the day, either he was at work or the kids were home.

I didn't like sleeping when the kids were home so I could be present in their lives. Eric wouldn't come home for a few hours after he got off work, and for a while, right at the time I needed to leave. But then he started coming home right away and acting like we were a happy family. On those nights, I would leave to work early and sleep in my car before work and after work so I could reduce the times I needed sleep at home as much as possible. He repulsed me.

Ren quickly got a job and bought a car. He needed that freedom, and I was so happy that he got a chance to pick up the pieces. He wouldn't talk much outside of basic conversations and schedule, keeping to himself most of the time. Through all this, I really became a helicopter parent, so fearful of the bad things that could happen. I was terrified of all the things that could harm the kids.

We went on like this for another year and a half, and I just couldn't take it any longer. The kids were old enough now and didn't seem to need me. Ren would graduate that spring, and the other two weren't far behind. Fights with Eric and me were bad and getting worse, but I couldn't divert him off the kids like before, and home could be a scary place. You couldn't look at a wall or door and not see the damage his rage met.

It was just before the holidays when something broke in me. I just couldn't go on with him. I looked online about divorce and learned a little about uncontested being a way to avoid lawyers and a lot of time. I went down to the courthouse asking how to file, paid a little money, and got a packet with some instructions and forms.

I filled out the forms, which included splitting assets, and simply wrote that we would sell everything and split it. I knew he wouldn't care if I had the kids, so I put that I would get full custody and he could have visitation whenever he wanted. I gave it to Eric after all the kids went to sleep, but he wouldn't look up from the tv. I told him to just sign, and we would both be out of our misery. He stopped briefly, like he was doing me a favor, and shuffled through the pages for a moment. Then looked back at the tv and said, "You're not going anywhere. You're not leaving me."

I kept pushing for him to sign. We didn't like each other; it was clear. Why wouldn't he sign? He came up with the excuse that he didn't want to sell everything. That gave me hope, so I re-wrote the terms. I said we could sell the house and then divide the things in it. He initially agreed but wouldn't sign.

The next morning, I called realtors about placing the house on the market. The same day, we had it listed. The agent gave me the estimated value, and I knew that would be enough to get out of under the loan and provide enough for us each to get another place. She told us that her guess of a sale would be in the spring, and with it being right before the holidays, it may sit for a little while, but sometimes after Thanksgiving and before Christmas, they see a little jump in sales. It just felt amazing to be moving forward.

Ren had a scholarship for college, and his future was looking bright. By the time the house sold, he would be near graduation and already said he planned to move out. I adjusted the divorce papers to include Trafton and Jessica and said to split the proceeds from the house sale. I went through an organized inventory of our belongings and who should get what. I tried to include Eric in this, but he always said later, but I wasn't going to wait for later.

The first week into December, I got the call that someone wanted to come view the house. I scrambled to get the dogs ready to leave and helped the kids make plans to hang out with friends. I anxiously waited for news after returning, but our realtor only said she let in the family and their realtor but has not heard anything back.

Two days later, they offered the full asking price! I said yes and hurried to call Eric so we could sign. This was the best news! I left a few messages for Eric but didn't hear back all day. Finally, when he came home, I hugged him and told him again. He flatly replied he is not signing. He doesn't agree to sell.

He now had my full attention and focus. I prepared him a plate of dinner from earlier that evening and sat with him trying to negotiate. He'd ask me for a drink, I'd get it. Then he'd ask for seconds, and I'd get it. I started to see that he was enjoying my desperate need for him at that moment, and I finally got up and walked away.

Hoping he would just give in, I waited but refused to beg and serve him. The agent called in the morning and gave us until the end of the day. Eric wouldn't sign. They ended up offering on another house.

Christmas Eve, he told me that he wanted to keep the house. I argued that without selling, I wouldn't be able to get another place. He gave a hint of a smile and walked away. I didn't think I could hate him more, but each day proved me wrong.

January, I proposed eleven more iterations of divorce papers. Each one relenting something else in his favor. He rejected them all. He would say things like, "if I don't sign, we aren't divorced" and "the state won't intervene for years, so we'll just see how you feel then". I had it! I wrote out one last stack of papers. He could have the house, all the things in the house, the timeshare, his 401(k), my 401(k), every penny we had - just let me go. He still said no.

He was getting everything and still refused. I told him that I didn't need the divorce, I was done, and I was leaving. I had to work that night and went upstairs to shower. As soon as I got out, I ran a basket of clothes downstairs that I wanted to have washed so I could pack them. When I got to the family room, all three kids were lined up sitting on the couch with Eric kneeling in front of them.

Jessica was bawling, Trafton was wiping tears from under his glasses, and Ren looked up, glaring at me. Eric turned when he saw Ren look up, and he had tears also. I asked what happened, and Eric turned away from the kids, standing now and looking right at me with a smirk and acting as if he was crying, said that he told them about my affairs.

I knew in that moment what he was doing. He wanted to turn the kids on me. He didn't think I would give him all our belongings, but when I did, he knew I wouldn't leave without the kids.

He said, "Tell the kids about why you are gone so long every night and about the guys you are sleeping with." I shouted back, "I'm working, there are no guys, I just can't stand to be with you!" I looked at the kids and laughed, saying that he is lying to you. Eric turned to the kids and said he has proof, pictures that he will show them.

Ren got up, saying he hates me, walking away and slamming his door behind him. Jessica ran past me to her room, crying, and Trafton wasn't far behind her, saying I am gross. I stood there holding my basket, looking at Eric, who turned to me with no tears now and said, "You want to leave? They won't go with you." He sat down and turned on the tv.

I dropped my basket and ran upstairs. Jessica was crying and looking out through a crack in the door, but when she saw me, she slammed her door. I tried knocking on both the kids' doors and said he was lying, but neither would open their doors to me.

In rage for Eric and full breakdown mode for what he had done, I went to my room, grabbing the bag I had pulled to pack my things, shoved my work clothes into it with extra clothes.

With tear-blinded eyes, I went downstairs with the bag and threw it on the chair by the front door. Screaming now at Eric that he is evil and there was nothing worse he could do but it wasn't going to work and I was not staying with him. Going back up to grab more things. I didn't know what I was going to do now, but I was not staying with him a second longer.

Up and down the stairs to put a pillow and blanket and coats and everything I could think of possibly needing on the chair. I was dressed enough to get out of there, my hair was sopping wet still, but I needed to leave. I could only think that I would go to work and sleep in my car and figure something out by morning.

Heading down the hall to the stairs, I see that Trafton's door is open, but he wasn't there. At the top of the stairs, I can hear Eric on the phone talking to someone about me. By the middle of the stairs, he tells the boys to stop me. Both Trafton and Ren have now pushed me down and are holding me. They are both bigger than I am, and I'm screaming for them to let me go. Eric hangs up the phone, opens the front door, and then helps them sit on me while I scream and fight to get loose.

NINETEEN

My head is throbbing, and I feel sick but can't stop the tears. Within moments, there are firemen in the house, dismissing my sons and grabbing me from the stairs, moving me to the living room couch.

There are now three firemen and four police in my living room, surrounding me. They are trying to get me to calm down, but I am on fire. I watch as one officer is following Eric up to the bedroom while I scream to have them let me go. I manage to calm down enough that I keep telling them that I'm trying to leave him, and he won't let me.

I get to a point that I'm trying to be calm so they will listen to me. The officers are asking my kids if I hurt them! I'm begging them to leave my kids out of this and keep repeating that I was going to leave him and want to divorce him, but he lied to the kids, and now I'm just trying to leave.

I point to my bag on the chair and say this over and over. Finally, the officers are telling the fireman that they have this handled, and they leave. There are now three officers left. One upstairs with Eric and two with me, and I keep telling them that I need to leave. That I will show them the divorce papers and just want to get away from him.

There is a short officer who seems to be in charge and keeps shouting at me to calm down. I'm now focused on this officer and telling him to let me go. I stood to head for the door, and he shoved me back so hard my head whipped back and hit the wall, and I knew I broke through the drywall. It felt like my head was cracked open. He shouted that I only move when he tells me to.

The other officer and Eric hear the commotion and come down the stairs. I can see Jessica peeking through her door in tears. I yell at Eric to call his bulldogs to get off me and that he is a coward. He walks straight to my bag, reaches in, and hands something to his officer.

I am threatened that if I move, I will be arrested. The officers gather around Eric, and I hear him say that I was planning to commit suicide with these pills. I laugh and say the only pills we have belong to him for his gout or kidney stones. I have no drugs! Eric is acting as if he is broken and worried for me. He tells them that I said I was going to kill myself, and he didn't know what else to do but get me help, and that is why he called for suicide protection. I yelled that if I was going to kill anyone, it would be him.

The short officer came right up to me, grabbed me by the arm, and in one swift motion stood me up, twisting me backward with my arm behind my back, and cuffed me! He got right up against my ear and said, "My ex-wife was just like you. You think you're too good for him?" I screamed out, "I'm just trying to leave him! I've never done drugs or drank alcohol, and he put those pills in my bag!"

We stood in the middle of the living room while everyone talked about me. My head hurt so bad I was only able to see directly in front of me. My ears were ringing, I was getting sick to my stomach, and my wrists hurt. In the calmest voice I could muster, I said, "I will go with you, just please take these off me. Please don't make me walk outside with these handcuffs. I haven't done anything wrong, and I don't want my neighbors to see me like this."

The short officer said, "You think these are too tight?" and he tightened them as hard as he could. Then he walked me to the front yard and stood with me there, saying that he would let everyone take a look at what I did to my family. The other officer gave his card to Eric and was told to go, that he would take me in. That officer got in his patrol car and drove away.

We stood in the yard while two of my neighbors came out to see if I was okay, but the short officer told them to stay back. I had tears and snot blanketing my face, but I couldn't wipe them away. I was moved to the backseat of the patrol car. He got in the front seat and started mocking me. Calling me names and saying that I would never recover my reputation as a good mom or wife. That Eric could do so much better than me.

He drove erratically, knowing that he was knocking me around this cold, hard bench, sliding and hitting my head on the door. I told him my head was hurting really badly and thought I might throw up. He threatened me if I messed up his car and turned up the radio so loud I thought my head would burst. I did everything I could to hold back what was trying to come up. I tried to duck down as all the cars near us were looking in my window.

I had no idea where we were going. How could I be arrested for trying to leave a marriage? We pulled under the awning of a hospital. I was met by two large male nurses who pulled me out of the car and through a waiting room. Everything stopped as I walked through, like a wave that quickly silenced the room. Only my sobbing could be heard.

The officer followed behind, and once we turned a corner and I was in a small room, a female nurse ran around the desk, telling the officer he could not go any further and to remove his cuffs. My arms were so sore, and I reached for my wrists, but they were too painful. I was in a hospital room, the door wide open, with these two large men telling me to disrobe. I protested and refused and was told that if I didn't do it, they would. I cried for so many reasons, not the least of which was my wrists ached, and I was humiliated. This could not be real.

As soon as my clothes dropped to the floor, one gathered them and moved them away quickly. The other put a gown over me and grabbed my arm, guiding me down the hall to a bathroom, telling me to pee in the cup. He stood in the doorway as the female nurse from before let me know that they had to watch to make sure it was my sample. They were drug testing me!

I was led back to the room. The nurse told me to sit on the bed and asked me why I was there. I told her the highlights of the evening while holding my wrists. She asked to take a look as I was bleeding and gently wrapped them up. She ran her hands along my wrists and asked what had happened, and I told her how he tightened them on me.

She let me know that I was brought there for a suicide watch. I told her that I wasn't committing suicide, had never taken drugs, and only wanted to leave the marriage. I was planning to go to work and needed to keep my job because I would never go back to him. She kindly said it was not up to her and that typically this is a 72-hour hold, but a doctor would be in to talk with me later. I was planning how I would stay calm and explain this whole thing, and the doctor would let me go.

My room was right next to the nurses' station. When she left, I heard her tell someone to x-ray my wrists as she thought the officer broke them. The door shut behind her. I was looking around this room and saw that everything had rounded edges and absolutely nothing was in the room but this bed with some paper I was sitting on. I used the bandages from my wrists to wipe my face dry.

I heard some voices outside the door about thirty minutes later. My door opened, and that evil little officer walked in with Eric and my kids! The nurse ran in and started screaming that they can't be here and who let you back. I was naked and embarrassed without the chance to speak with the kids. My door slammed, and muffled yelling was heard. Then silence.

Another hour went by, per my best estimates. They took my watch, and there were no clocks in the room, so this was my best guess. The door opened, and a tall male doctor came in, leaving the door open behind him. He was wheeling in his own stool and sat on it in front of me. He asked my name and birthdate, introduced himself, and proceeded to tell me that he had just visited with my husband in the waiting room. Any hope I had of him hearing my side was gone. Eric would lie, but I would look crazy to them.

He summarized what Eric shared and then asked me what had happened. I talked so fast, afraid that he would stop me without hearing it all and pass his judgement, not allowing me to leave. I ended by saying that he was trying to keep me here so he knew where I was. He was controlling, and I was scared of what he would do to me.

The doctor rolled back on his stool and said, "We see this too often. I could see through his fake tears and story. He stopped you from leaving him and now knows exactly where you are and that you cannot leave for 72 hours at least. Do you have a safe place you can go?"

Relief spread through my body, and I knew he could see this too. I told him that I needed to go to work and that I would be safe there. I couldn't lose my job but would figure something out between now and then. He offered some safe houses he could connect me with, but I insisted that I needed to work. He helped me work out a plan to get my car dropped off and asked if I had anyone I could call. I didn't have anyone and definitely didn't have any numbers memorized that weren't my kids.

He helped me call information to get the number to a friend from church, and he spoke with her, saying that I was injured and needed my car and purse dropped off at the hospital. He then called Eric and told him that I would need these, and he made arrangements for when I was discharged and assured him that they would be holding me for the 72 hours. The doctor said he preferred if I go to a safe house, but he is not holding me.

He warned me, saying that after the 72 hours, Eric would be back looking for me. My clothes were brought in, and while waiting for the car to be dropped off, the nurse talked to me about filing charges against the officer. I said yes, and she helped write down what happened, which I signed and dated. She said that all domestic issues forbid the other party from knowing where I was taken and would get my statement to the right people. She hugged me and said how sorry she was and hoped I had a safe place to go.

TWENTY

I walked around the large parking lot for a while and finally found my car. The bag I had left on the chair that day was stuffed under the back seat. I shuffled through it to find some of the clothes I had packed, but you could tell it had been gone through. My purse was in it, but my ID was missing from the wallet, and all the cash was gone. I only had my debit card and two checks from my business account. My phone was dead, and I had no charger. No coat or jacket, and it was snowing.

    I drove quickly to work, changing clothes in the car so I wouldn't be late. It would be a miracle if I made it on time. I tried to fix my hair and face and pulled my sleeves low to cover my bruised and sore wrists. I told myself to hold it together and would figure out what to do next after work. It was my Friday, so I just needed to make it through the night. I was shattered for my children and in full rage for Eric, but right now, I needed to hold myself together.

    When I got into work, I was able to borrow a charger and left my phone in the break room to charge. I went through the lost and found closet and found a coat I could wear. In conversation, I mentioned to a co-worker that I was definitely leaving

Eric now. She knew that I had been unhappy, but the last we talked, I told her I was stuck and couldn't leave. I didn't tell her what had just happened, though.

I'm not sure if it is pure embarrassment, shame, or not having any answers. She was excited for me and told me we should celebrate after work, and I agreed. She wanted me to come to her place and knew I could come up with an excuse to stay the night. About an hour later, I went back to my phone, but I couldn't make a call, so I asked my friend to call me, and she held her phone out so I could hear that this number has been disconnected. He disconnected my phone!

As we were leaving work, I was to follow her but told her I needed to stop for gas. I went to swipe my debit card, but the reader said "see attendant". I went inside, but they couldn't run the card either. My friend saw me inside the station and used her card to fill my tank. When I came out in tears, she closed the gas door and said to follow her walking away.

I was screaming to myself the whole drive. All the things I hoped Eric could feel from me and the vengeance I was going to take on him. He was not going to get away with this! When we got to her house, I immediately promised repayment. She brushed me off and took me on a tour of her home. One of the rooms we passed, she said, would be for me. We worked the same days, so she insisted I hang out for the weekend. We stayed up late listening to music while her husband kept bringing her drinks and me snacks.

When morning came, I was anxious to get to the bank to figure out what was going on and pull out cash and to pay her back for the gas. My mind was reeling on all the evil things Eric was doing to me. I got to the bank and showed them my debit card to ask why it wasn't working. They asked for my ID, and I tried to explain that I didn't have it. After a manager was called, I was finally told that my husband had called to say that my purse was stolen. I needed to get my ID so they could help me order a new debit card. Even if I had an ID, this would be mailed to the house.

I asked if I could pull some cash, but without the ID, they couldn't help me. I remembered the checks from my business account but was told the same thing. He had gotten the bank to freeze any ability I had to access funds. I tried to explain this, but they said I needed an ID, birth certificate, passport... something to show my identification. Everything was at the house. He was trying to force me back to him. I waited to speak with the manager as I'm sure I'm not the first person to have a spouse manipulate financial accounts but got no where. They were kind but their hands were tied. To restrict accounts just takes a call but to untangle it feels impossible.

In my car, I cried, yelled, slept, and begged God for help. Or vengeance. As the night and cold set in, I could only return to her house again. I didn't want to stay up all night but needed a place to stay, so each night I grew more and more exhausted. By the end of my weekend, I had no choice but to call him.

I called from her house, and he answered, not recognizing the number. I was silent for a moment, but he knew it was me. He started crying that he had been worried and that they all missed me and wanted me home. I simply replied, "I will never come back to you and will be coming by for my things in forty-five minutes, and I want you gone." I hung up before he could respond.

The drive home was a flip-flop between my utter hatred for Eric and concern for the kids. If it was just Eric, I would plow through him and get my things and never look back. Maybe the kids would come with me? Anger and intense sadness pulled my tears from streaming down my face to stone coldness where they weren't able to leave my eyes.

When I pulled up to the house, I was sick to see his car there but knew what I needed to do. ID, clothes, coats, toiletries, shoes, blankets, all the documents I could grab....He was waiting for me and opened the door, reaching for me like he thought I would let him hug me. I pushed past him and charged for my bedroom. The kids were home but were not coming to me.

Eric followed me to the bedroom and sat at the foot of the bed, watching me for a moment but then said that if I leave him or stop my paychecks from depositing into the bank, he would stop the mortgage payment and the kids would be on the street. He continued to say that even if I do get my ID, the money isn't in that account anymore. He also said that he wasn't able to reach me by phone and that there must have been a misunderstanding, but he fixed it.

I pretended not to listen but was feeling defeated. Not allowing him to see my face, I kept shoveling things into my too-small bag and charged past him. Down the stairs, I turned to where I heard the kids and pleaded with them, saying their father lied to them and I have been the only one who has been with them and cared for them. How could you believe him over me? They just looked at me as Eric was quickly behind me. So I turned and ran out the door, driving away afraid he would try to physically stop me.

I had managed to grab about eighty dollars from the nightstand. I don't know how I didn't get into an accident as I was speeding through tears back to my friend's house to repay her. They insisted that I stay with them and led me to the room, allowing me to just hide there for the next couple of days.

My cell phone was back on, so I called in sick to work. I left my sister a message asking if I could visit her and the family, not telling her any details. She texted me later saying that she was on vacation and no one was home. I texted back that Eric and I were having some problems and I just needed to get away, so she offered me to stay at her place. I had barely enough cash to get a one-way flight out. I had never done anything like this before and never without my children. She was concerned, but I didn't give her much information, just profusely thanking her.

About a week went by, and I knew I needed to return to work. All my ideas had piddled to nothing, and I didn't know what to do. I texted Eric, "What do you want from me?" He quickly replied, "A call." I sat on a kitchen stool looking out the window and called him. I didn't say a word, but after a moment, he told me he knew where I was from the online phone records. That his conditions were that I had to come back. If I did, he agreed to file the last iteration of divorce papers where he gets everything and will rewrite it showing that he filed as the petitioner, but I have to live with him until the divorce is final.

Ninety days. And I had to go with him to the counselor he picked out. Once the divorce was final, he would help me move out. I just sat there in the silence. I knew he was waiting for my reply. I hated him and was so confused at his conditions. Did he think I was going to go to counseling with him and change my mind? Has he lost his mind? I just ended the call.

So many things raced through my head. I would be with the kids and still work overnight away from Eric. He would file for the divorce. It would be final about the same time Ren graduates. What other options do I have?

An hour later, I texted him that I needed money to fly back. He bought the ticket and emailed the confirmation with a note that he loved me. Sick!

Before I left, I opened a new email address and looked up how to obtain a PO Box. All my employment had been temporary jobs that had no benefits. At this moment, I wished I had prioritized my own money and career. I was financially dependent on this sick monster. If it weren't for the children, I would never return. And he knew that.

TWENTY ONE

I gave myself a pep talk several times a day. Rehearsing how I would be happy and present for the kids and silently planning how to leave for work before Eric had a chance to come home first. I resented Eric for putting the kids in the middle of our issues and refused to do that to them. If they wanted to talk, I was open, and if they wanted to avoid the topic, I would let them. I don't know what else Eric had been feeding them; I knew there was more, but I needed to put their needs before my concerns.

Ren stayed as distant as he could. It wasn't too hard with him working most nights after school. Our conversations revolved around his upcoming graduation and the letters of scholarships from colleges received. Trafton seemed torn, as there were times he just wanted to be with me and struggled with the stories he was told. I felt like he wanted to talk, but something would stop him. Jess appeared to be back to her happy self. The air always changed when Eric and I were home at the same time. The kids would find reasons to scatter.

It had taken another two weeks for him to finally give me the envelope of papers he had re-filled out for my signature. He swore he would file them at the courthouse. He said that three different times, but I would purposely walk past his car to check the mail just to peer inside to see if the envelope was still sitting on the passenger seat. There it was.

Not wanting to start another war but only here because of his promise to file, I decided that a direct approach was not a language he responded well to, so I left a bag with some clothes in it near my dresser, hoping he would see it and think I was planning to leave. It worked. He gave me the envelope with excuses on why he hadn't been able to go.

I had the biggest smile on my face and tears in my eyes when my number was called, and they took the paperwork and filing fee and set the date for ninety days. As long as the divorce was uncontested, we just had to wait out the clock. He was still getting everything, but I would be free of him, and that was worth it all. The immense relief and anticipation that the countdown was truly official fueled me to finally dream of a life without him.

I started looking at the apartments that were within walking distance from the high school. Checking out the amenities the kids might like. I asked about rent and the deposit but didn't dare pull the money out of the account until I could make this Eric's idea. They let me know that I would need to reserve a place months before they became available. I dreamed of the kids and their friends at the pools and having barbecues. There were two gyms and a clubhouse with a pool table and foosball... I was imagining a happy new beginning.

As agreed, I went to Eric's chosen counselor, which was a joke. I didn't like him, love him, or respect him, but I did fear his temper tantrums. There was absolutely no way in hell I would reconcile with him. I said this over again, but it finally hit him one day after his one-on-one with the counselor, who said the same thing. That set him off. I was upstairs dressing for my late shift, and he came raging in, screaming about how I am wasting his money, pretending like I was working on our marriage.

I picked up the pace of what I was doing and remarked that I never said that; this was just part of his conditions. He put his fist through the wall, cleared the dresser top of anything on it, threw whatever he could in my direction, opened and slammed the door repeatedly, but I just gathered my things like I didn't know I was supposed to be afraid.

That fueled him even more as he was losing control over me. Then the names started. He called me a whore, cheater, bitch, and all the ugly names I could not repeat. I managed to run past him to the door before he could stop me and ran down the stairs. Trafton grabbed Jessica and pulled her into his room, shutting the door quickly. Ren yelled up to Eric, asking if he wanted him to "stop the bitch." I turned and looked right at Ren. He had never talked like that.

I looked behind me at Eric and said, "Look what you've done." Ren started laughing and said that

I always told him to speak the truth, and Eric is right that I'm a whore. I went to my car and drove away. When I turned out of the neighborhood, the tears flooded my face, and I couldn't find my breath.

The next couple of months, I tried so many ways of getting money to hide, but Eric was watching me closely, and my only source of income was my paycheck that was direct-deposited. I couldn't ask anyone for help as they didn't know what was going on, and I couldn't risk anything being this close to the end. The name-calling was now daily, with both Eric and Ren feeding off each other.

The apartment manager knew I was getting divorced and had a pretty good idea what I was dealing with when I told her I needed him to agree to pulling the deposit out of the bank. When she would tell me when the month's rent had to be paid, I asked her to email that to me so it would come from the apartments and not me. I would text Eric during my overnight hours in hopes he was sleeping and wouldn't respond right away.

I tried to make it seem like I was asking or looking for his permission, knowing how not to bait him. I forwarded the email and told him I needed to pull the funds out on my way home and pay the rent. He didn't respond, so I hurried before anything could happen.

I told him that my schedule still works around the kids so they could come to my place after school and on his days (because now he acted like he needed at least half-time with them), he could pick them up after work. To make sure there was no question around the kids being with me or having Eric put them in a position to choose, I worked out a schedule with Trafton so we could share my car. Slow and steady seemed to work!

We were down to about a month to the court date, and I was feeling on top of the world, even though Eric was getting more angry every day. I had been with Eric since I was eighteen. Now eighteen years later, and I was so excited to be the one deciding my future. Late one night, he sent a text listing how things were going to go. He said that we would go to the court together and afterward go to breakfast. Then he would allow me to move out with his help (meaning he would be in my apartment). I could have the living room couch, a bed, a dresser, and my piano. I thanked him, allowing him to feel in control a moment longer.

Ren graduated and moved out to his own apartment complex across the road from mine a week before our court date. He decided to take time off before going to university. I took Trafton and Jessica over to the apartments to show them the amenities and get them excited for the upcoming change. They genuinely seemed excited too. Their friends could come over after school also to swim and play pool anytime, and they really liked the new life that was taking shape.

I overheard Eric talking on his phone, telling the other party that he was okay because I was going through something and even if I went through with the divorce, I would come back.

As agreed, we drove together to the courthouse. We sat before the judge, who had questions about why I wasn't asking for child support or spousal support, and he was getting everything. Eric insisted on holding my hand. I don't know if it was because I could taste freedom or was afraid the judge would order us to take time and change the settlement, but I just said we agreed this was best.

He challenged me a couple of times, trying to help me I'm sure, but I was shaking as I couldn't take one more minute in this marriage and begged him to allow it through. He did. We were divorced! I even got so excited I hugged Eric. This must have looked so strange to the judge.

Finally, I was moving. Eric hung out at my place almost the entire day. I didn't know when I could kick his sorry ass out and know I was free from worrying about his triggers. I learned that as long as the kids were still home, to some degree, we would play this game.

I was not making it month to month but refused to change my job as the shift worked for Trafton and Jessica nicely. I enrolled back into school to finish the degree Eric wouldn't support. I spoke with a retired accountant who outlined costs and speed of graduation, and I nervously scheduled the screening exams.

I worked out the schedule where Trafton would take my car, drop me off at the nearby bus stop, and bus to the train station headed downtown. He would then drive himself and Jessica to school. When my classes were done, I would take the train back to the bus station and walk the two miles home before they got out of school. I was excited and felt tremendous gratitude that I could do this and show the kids the importance of a higher education.

In addition to finishing school, I wanted to listen to country music and dance. Two things he said no to while we were married. I found a dance hall that had free line dancing classes on an early Wednesday night and went alone. This was my first time in a club or a dancing class. It was summer, so I wore a pair of shorts, a t-shirt, and tennis shoes. I was so far out of my comfort zone but refused to let my fears stop me. Even though my feet stuck to the floor, I had so much fun and met new friends.

I ended up joining a fairly large group of friends who would go dancing or get together often. This suited me well as I could go when I wanted or was able, but if I needed to leave, I wasn't breaking up the party. This became a separate world from the one at home where I was struggling. These friends knew I was recently divorced and had children, but otherwise, I didn't share much and just enjoyed their company.

At home, I was so happy to have the kids and their friends over constantly. I managed to have the kids over every day, even on days they were supposed to be with Eric. I said they could be with me until he got home from work. Since he rarely came home when work ended, I had the kids a lot and loved it so much. Unfortunately, when Eric did come to pick up the kids, instead of texting them to head out, he would come in and join us for dinner or whatever we were doing. I tried to push the kids to watch for him but was afraid to jeopardize them being with me every day. I knew this was some game he was playing, but right now, I was the one benefiting the most.

Eric had agreed that he would help with food for the kids and gas as they were using my car, but he would not agree to put any of this in the settlement agreement. It had been some months, and I really needed some help, so I asked through a text. He agreed that he could give a little, but he had conditions. Of course, he did. He decided that $45.00 a week was sufficient, but he would only do this if he went shopping with me. I didn't feel like I had another option, so I agreed, and since I cooked everything at home, I made $45.00 stretch pretty far. Two teenagers and him many nights was absurd, but he needed to feel in control.

After a couple of months of having to shop with Eric while he acted like we were still a family, I told him that my schedule was making it too difficult to continue. He said that giving me money felt like he was paying me to divorce him. I hated that I needed anything from him and laughed to myself that he was acting like these scraps were such a generous gift. He knew I was strapped, and he loved the power he still had. He said he needed time to think about this.

Two days later, I received a text that he would do the shopping and drop food off at my place, saving me the trip, and that he would need a key. With my low pay, school fees, and other modest bills, I agreed. He bought trash food. Premade cinnamon rolls full of frosting for breakfast and other food I would never feed the kids. He ignored my attempts at sending shopping lists of flour, pasta, rice, and other cooking staples, saying he was making it easier for me. When I would get home, I could tell he had gone through my room and my dresser. Specifically my panty drawer. I couldn't do this anymore.

TWENTY TWO

I asked my bishop if we could talk and explained to him what was going on. My bishop could talk to our old bishop (or Eric's bishop, but he couldn't tell me what was being said, nor did I care. I was so exhausted from my work and school schedule, making sure the kids always had a present mom. My bishop was turning red and told me to immediately change my locks.

He had been telling me to defend myself every time we met, and I would only reply that I'm not putting my kids in the middle of anything and I didn't know what "defend" myself would even look like. I knew that he told them I was having affairs, but they could see I was with them all the time and always had been. They would know the truth someday without me thrusting them in the middle.

My bishop got so upset with my carefree attitude and told me there were many horrible things he was saying. He even walked over to me one time, grabbed both of my shoulders, shook me saying, "Defend yourself!" It startled me, and I knew he knew things I didn't, but I was not going to do anything to upset our situation and felt so confident that one day, the kids would know the truth and that I loved them so much that I put them before my need to clear my name.

Changing my locks did it for Eric. No more help. No more pretend kindness. I could tell he was trying to turn the kids against me again. It didn't take long for Jessica to start pulling away and saying awful things. She got physical one time and refused to come to my place. Trafton said he was sorry but needed to go with her to protect her. My attempts to text and call the kids went unanswered. Trafton came by once telling me that they were not allowed to use their phones to talk to me, and Eric was watching the call logs and hurried away afraid that Eric would know he came to see me. They were with me only a year before I lost them.

Devastated, I can't express my sadness. I poured myself into my courses, working hard to graduate as soon as I could. I was taking thirty credit hours in the summer while working. I had to get special permissions, but I needed this badly and don't remember sleeping. I told myself that Ren pulled away from me because I was the only one who really knew what he had been through, and he wanted a life without any memory of that. I told myself that Jessica and Trafton got sucked into the controlling lies of Eric. Someday, somehow, they would understand and come back. I just knew it. I needed to believe this.

As soon as I graduated, I got in my car and drove. I couldn't handle the whirlwind in my mind now that my studies didn't occupy my every thought.

Knowing how geographically close the kids were, but I couldn't see them, tore me apart. I wanted so badly to escape the pain, and running away seemed to confuse my mind enough to distract me. I was really a private person but also didn't want anyone to think badly of my children, so I didn't even share with my family. I just headed for the mountains.

After a day of driving, I decided that I would reach out to family and say I was coming for a quick visit. Claire was the only one who replied and said that they were looking forward to it. Although I wasn't close with my family, we were on decent terms, so I drove to her house and arrived the following day. I just said I was camping and traveling after graduation. I adore her kids, and so we just played for a couple of days when Claire asked when I would be leaving.

I thanked her, hugging the kids and saying it was time for me to head back. Before leaving, my oldest niece said that she was the star in the school play and hoped I would come back for that. I told her I would try.

I drove back to Colorado but felt so lost and like I was imploding, so I drove back to Claire's again the following week, using the play as the excuse. I stayed again for two days when my brother Byron called. He saw our niece post about her play and who was there. Byron couldn't believe I would come so far and not see him. I honestly didn't know he was near, and we agreed to meet for dinner the next day.

Byron knew something was wrong, and he pushed. I cried out parts of my story, and he just swept me under his wing. He had recently gotten divorced and moved into a large place with his kids. He brought me to his home and showed me a room and bathroom that were closed off since they didn't need them and insisted I stay there.

I drove back to Colorado and gathered my things and stayed with Byron. I didn't know what my next move was, but having him and his sweet kids to dote on really saved me. At a month, I found work and moved into my own place in the same community. It was nice to have family near. I hadn't lived near family since I was a teen but told everyone this was just temporary.

That May, I received a text from Trafton with a graduation invitation picture and immediately called him, but when he answered, he only said, 'Dad doesn't know I told you' and hung up. I was so excited and made plans to be there, of course. With my arms full of gifts, I made my way to the graduation, rehearsing how I wouldn't cry and would make sure he wouldn't feel anything but love from me. No sadness for his big day.

I was sitting so far away and could barely make him out walking to the stage, screaming for him but knowing he would never hear me. Hours went by while I looked for him and texted him in the massive crowds gathering for pictures. I walked everywhere looking for him. He never returned my texts. Defeated when the crowds thinned to nothing, I made my way back to the car. Staying in a Walmart parking lot just in case he reached out— but nothing.

At the end of the summer, Trafton reached out to me, saying he wanted to see me, so I drove back and met him for dinner. He didn't know where I was, and we spent some time catching up. His hug carried the weight of so much sadness, but I refused to let this be about anything but joy. He shared that things weren't great and he worried Dad would find out he came to see me.

He told me that he had a girlfriend and thoughts about his future. I soaked him in and said that I was here for him anytime. I offered a phone and other support, but he said Dad would find out. I was sick and angry at the situation but didn't want to push him away, so I held my anger for later when I was alone.

He ended up coming out for a visit the next month, and I arranged a big family day on the lake. Everyone was excited to see him too, and we had a really great visit. Wakeboarding and cousins. The door was open whenever he wanted, and I made sure he knew that. He told me that he wanted to move to Seattle and was making plans.

I made visits back there almost every month. Byron came with me once, and Claire another time. I got to see both Trafton and Ren but never Jessica. She just refused. I was filled with hope for a bright future.

I even met someone on a dating app. He came off as arrogant, which I didn't like, but funny. He asked to call, and we had a short conversation, leaving us both laughing, so we agreed to meet. My initial impression when I saw him wasn't great. He looked older than his pictures, had less hair, and was wearing some mismatched gym clothes. I was dressed in my cute pink shorts with a polka-dot top and wedges. He didn't even try.

It was a beautiful day, so we agreed to walk around the lake. No big commitment, and it was nice to be out. But I was already thinking of how I would say a polite goodbye before we got back to the parking lot so I could jump in the car and leave before things got uncomfortable.

By the time we were only halfway around the lake, I was really into this guy. His 'game' wore off fast, and I got to hear this funny and kind guy emerge. I've never not felt an attraction at the start, and it turned. Now, I'm so attracted. We spent so much time there. Something special was happening between us. Our banter and connection were electrifying. It wasn't just that he turned out to be a great guy but that together, our collective energy really shined. After a couple of trips around the lake, I was anticipating a hug when we got to the parking lot as the evening set in.

When we weren't together, we were talking on the phone or texting. We talked about our kids, beliefs, life, and things just seemed incredible when we were together. Lots of laughter and a thrill in the air. I hadn't felt quite this way in some time.

His kids were younger than mine. I thought his setup was odd, but what I had certainly wasn't ideal, so I didn't judge. The kids lived with his ex, but they were with Rob every other weekend and many days after work. When his kids weren't with him, he was with me. The second week after meeting, he asked me to go to a soccer practice with his son. I was excited as this told me he wanted me to be a part of his life and introduce me to his kids. It seemed kind of quick, but I was in!

Rob came to my place to pick me up with his son and a friend in the backseat in their team uniforms. There was a quick introduction, and while I was getting my seatbelt on, Rob reached over and squeezed my hand. I felt so happy. I got the feeling that he was as into me as I was to him. As we turned out of my neighborhood, his son asked if I was the same Tina that dated Cliff.

What!? A shot of confusion came over me quickly, and I looked over at Rob trying to understand this question. His son was directly behind me, so I couldn't see him, but I never mentioned Cliff to Rob before.

Byron and I hung out in a large singles group since moving here. We played volleyball, and there were always tons of events. Cliff was hanging around Byron a lot, and that is how we met. He was a muscle man and the hottest guy in the group. I was told that

Byron was in this category with him. All the girls swooned over them. I admit he was gorgeous, but I never set my sights on him or any other guy. I just enjoyed the fun and distractions this group provided.

Over time, though, Cliff was heavily pursuing me, and we started dating. All the girls were jealous that I had both my brother and Cliff around. We dated a little on our own, but most of the time, we were together in this large group, so I had my brother and girlfriends too. This was kind of my first boyfriend, and it was exciting.

Within a couple of months, I got to really know Cliff, and he was just a guy who peaked in high school, and there was really nothing else to him. He talked about his glory football days and his muscles. The stories of his success were nothing more than exaggerations and embellishments. It was hard to hold any meaningful conversation with him, but while we were with our collective friends and playing, he was the life of the party and a blast to be with.

TWENTY THREE

Cliff got serious quickly, but I just never thought of him as more than a fun guy to date and told him so as nicely as I could. Honestly, I think he was just looking for someone to provide for him. He would endlessly flirt with other girls to try and make me jealous. Then he would show up at my door and ask me to forgive him. I didn't feel any deep feelings for him and broke things off. He didn't take it well, and I would hear rumors of things he would tell others to save face. Just what you'd expect in high school.

Anyway, back to the car with Rob's sons' question. Confused on how he knew to ask this question, I answered that yes, I had dated him before. I asked where he heard this, and he said his mom told him to ask me. I looked again at Rob, trying to read his face and this whole conversation. He only shrugged and kept driving.

After practice, Rob dropped off his son and was taking me home when I burst into asking who his ex was and why she would tell his son to ask this of me. Rob would laugh and say he had no idea, but by the time we reached my place, he let me know that he and his ex tell each other things about who they are dating for the kids' sake, and she must have known of me, but it was no big deal.

I had never heard of her, and she definitely didn't play volleyball or spend time in our large group. I was mostly upset because Cliff became very mean and jealous and tried hard to spread hurtful gossip about me.

Rob didn't seem affected by any of it and kissed me when he dropped me off. When I got inside, I started searching for her in the groups online chats and found her. There didn't seem to be anything that stood out, but I did see her in many of the singles' group chat threads we were in. She responded often to posts from Cliff over the past several months, hearting everything he said, and seemed to be flirting with him, trying to get his attention. Cliff didn't respond to her in these posts, and I gathered that she was one of his many groupies. I shook it off and went to sleep dreaming of Rob and the feelings I was having for him.

Rob and I just got closer. I spent time with his kids often now, and although they were the most spoiled and entitled kids, I just imagined what I would do to my kids if I had the means. I had always loved children, and my feelings for Rob were getting so strong. When they were around, all our focus was on them—as it should be.

The times it was just us, wow. I couldn't get over how amazing it felt and how we just seemed to bring out the best in each other. From being playful to serious conversations, we just seemed to blend in the best ways.

There were other questions from his kids to me about things only privately shared between Rob and me as time went on. Questions about why my kids weren't with me and worded in ways I learned were coming from his ex. There were comments about my age when I had my kids with judgments that were harsh and cold. It's hard to explain, but you could tell these questions weren't coming from children. They were being re-told and prompted.

From the beginning, I questioned Rob's relationship with his ex and told him that when I shared intimate information about my children, that was only between us. He pushed back that I just didn't know what it was like to not have a contentious relationship with my ex and that it was good for the children. I agreed with him to a point and understood there are degrees of divorce, but he kept assuring me that they were only co-parents and he had no other feelings for her.

I didn't feel that he had feelings for her, but what about her feelings for him? He reminded me that she left him. She wanted attention from other men, so there really was nothing for me to worry about.

We lived about forty-five minutes away from each other. He either stayed with me or I stayed with him unless his kids were around. He shared that he needed to stay near his ex so it was easier to be with his kids. He told me he loved me and asked me to move closer to him. I felt really excited but didn't know that this was love quite yet but said it back anyway. If this wasn't love, it would be soon enough.

We hadn't known each other too long, but I didn't even hesitate, and within a short time, I moved into the same neighborhood as him, just about twelve townhomes away. We were living together, but he made sure no one knew that part, which, in a heavily religious area, I understood. Neither of us was actively religious but still understood the judgment.

Four months later, on a Saturday morning in his kitchen, we were talking, and he asked me to marry him. No ring or down on one knee, and it shocked me. I stared at him for a bit and realized he was serious! He moves fast, but I was crazy for him and hoped this is where it would lead at some point anyway. I hugged him so tight and said yes! I never thought I would marry again, but I didn't want to be without him and loved the idea of not pretending to live separately.

We had a blissful weekend, just soaked in the idea of a life together. I felt positive that this was my second chance at love and that everything was happening as it should and was meant to be.

We told his kids together, his dad, and my siblings. Everyone was happy for us. As the week went on though, I heard about some things I didn't understand. Rob always shrugged things off, so my growing questions didn't seem to faze him. His kids were acting differently, and I was hearing pieces of rumors from the singles groups about me. I hadn't been active in these groups after meeting Rob, but they were still my friends.

Rob would have me watch his youngest while he carpooled the others sometimes, and I would hear a little something here and there that didn't feel good, but I couldn't put my finger on anything concrete. When I would share things about this with Rob, he would just hug me and tell me not to worry. I struggled a bit with his kids and their demands and Rob's bending to whatever they wanted but told myself things can't be perfect and counted the years before it would be just the two of us.

A friend from the singles group called me one night and told me some things he had heard. They were about my kids and most specifically about my daughter. There were also rumors about my kids not wanting anything to do with me, and that I was a teen mom. I didn't share any of this with anyone as I have always been so protective of my children and myself. No one would have known these things as I lived out of state.

This wasn't just a little thing. It was a big, horrible, personal thing, and apparently, everyone in this large group had now heard it. I was reeling and tearful. So confused. The only person I shared this with was Byron and Rob. Byron would never say these things, and Rob wasn't a part of the singles group. I couldn't understand and couldn't sleep for days.

When Rob and I were together again after a long weekend away with his kids, I confided in him about my devastation and confusion. He listened but acted as confused as I was. After some time and wiping away my tears, I pulled away from his embrace and asked him if he had shared this with anyone. He admitted that he had told his ex.

What? Why? Why was he talking about me and why such intimate things? And why with her? Why was she spreading rumors about my children? What was going on between them? Where did he get off thinking he could tell others about our personal conversations and about my kids? He only defended her and said he knew she wasn't the one to tell others and it must have been my brother. We got into a big fight, and I broke off the engagement.

Over the next several days, he would text and call and come to the house, but I wouldn't respond. He was apologizing and leaving flowers and making promises. I missed him so much and opened my door to him about a week later. Although we weren't engaged now, we slid back into our relationship.

His older girls especially were treating me differently and became rude and irritated around me. There were times when they were around that I would go hide in a closet. I overheard them talking about the kind of girl I was having a kid with so young. I just didn't know what to do, and my efforts to bond with them were rejected. Rob just told me to give them time.

I started to dread being around while they were there, not knowing what kind of day we were going to have. All we did when the kids were around was cater to their schedules and demands on Rob anyway. As soon as I had time with just Rob, all my concerns would wash away. We just had something so wonderful together, and I didn't want anything to ruin it.

I didn't understand why Rob would pick up and drop off the kids at their mom's house almost daily but didn't want them to live half-time with him. It seemed like he enjoyed being the fun parent without the responsibilities, and his ex seemed to like the spousal and child support. After this rumor thing, Rob would do his pickups without me more and more. I would question him a lot. Not just a general "what is going on" but "what is going on between you and your ex". I would ask very direct and pointed questions about the time he would spend with her at the house he bought her after the divorce and to let me know if something was going on.

He would laugh and grab me close and say I was cute when I was jealous. That made me mad as I had never been a jealous person before but felt he wasn't being honest with me. He would always find ways to make me believe I just didn't understand the co-parenting relationship. He hit a spot that I couldn't argue as I really didn't, but my gut told me there were things I didn't know.

Rob confided that while he was in college, a relationship he had with a girl strictly for sex ended in a pregnancy, but they decided to abort. He shared this to let me know that he didn't judge me, but I struggled not to judge him. He let me know that he didn't tell anyone, so no one knew but his ex. I asked why he didn't talk to his daughters about the things they were saying about me, and he just brushed it off as they were repeating what their mom was saying. I told him that he should talk to them about this, but he never did.

So he was living with me but didn't want anyone to know. He aborted a baby but didn't want anyone to know. They could attack me, but his reputation was protected. Was he working to protect my reputation like he said?

We would fight about her. We broke up and got back together many times. He would tell me that he knew she would sleep with him anytime he let her, but he would never do that, and I was all he wanted. He shared that his oldest daughter said that her mom was flirting with him, and it was gross. The little I knew of her was that she was constantly trying to get attention from everyone. I could see it in her comments and behavior in the singles groups. She would phish for compliments and always try to position herself in the center of everything.

Rob shared that she had left him, and they were not a good match, and he had no attraction or feelings for her. I tried to believe that she was just heavily pursuing him because she wanted to be wanted but believed Rob when he said I was the only one for him.

His ex and Cliff had now been spending a lot of time together. His kids would share what they would talk about—me. Me. They couldn't get my name out of their mouths, and both were actively putting me down and talking about my kids and trying to warn his children about me. Why was she so hateful? She left him years before and didn't want him, outside of his money, until now. This wasn't a new breakup for them, and I certainly wasn't the cause of it but seemed to be a focus for her.

TWENTY FOUR

We continued to date, break up, and get back together again. One breakup happened the night before my birthday. The conversation was so strange that I said it just seemed like he wanted to break up but didn't have a reason. He said yes, so I told him to leave. Within a week or so, he was back. He would come with me to Colorado to visit my boys. Trafton came out often now for visits.

My boys met Rob's kids, and I never told anyone how often we would split. Even with all that, it felt like things were going to work out somehow. Whenever it was just the two of us, it really did feel like we had something rare and special.

Around two years together, he proposed again, and I said yes again. Still no ring and no formal event. He was all I wanted and got excited, feeling like the previous engagement was too early in our relationship, but now we were ready. Rob wasn't like any other guy I knew when it came to planning a wedding. He knew what he wanted and the type of dress he wanted me to wear. He wanted the big ceremony and planned to invite all his clients. I knew how expensive this could be, and he replied that we could make a lot of money that would easily cover the expenses.

Since we had both been married before and my kids weren't around, I suggested a destination wedding in Hawaii. Neither of us had been, and we could have a magical ceremony on the beach together. He loved the idea, and that weekend, we went shopping for rings and dreaming up plans. He really wanted his kids there, and I knew I wouldn't have all of mine present, feeling sadness but agreeing.

I suggested that they would come out with us and play for a day before the wedding, and the day after the wedding, they would fly home, and we would continue our honeymoon there. We were excited and laughing and making plans online. We were writing out the costs and deciding what my 50% would be, as my budget was much tighter. I needed to know this so we could pick a date.

I always paid half of everything and was fine with that. Sometimes, he would feel embarrassed in public, although he insisted on this, and would pay but have me reimburse him once we left wherever we had been. He had bragged about how much money he made as a financial advisor, so I didn't doubt him. He seemed to want his kids to feel like rich kids and gave them anything and everything, but he lived very meagerly. Renting a small place with an old car.

We were at a weekend where he had his kids and busy schedules, so I asked for that time alone. I had so much to do to plan our wedding. I was so grateful to marry the love of my life and create a magical and intimate ceremony on the beach. I so strongly believed that all the heartache life had for me had brought me to this place, and I finally found a person that was home for me. I had been finding hotels and companies who offered beach weddings and sorting through reviews to pick the best places to visit. I excitedly wanted to share all the information I had gathered for our special moment. He was excited too about the plans and all the work I had done.

Rob and I were alone together the following weekend, and I shared that I had found flights and needed to pin down the day. He got serious and wanted to talk. After he had shared the news about our plans with his kids (with his ex present), he would only go to Hawaii if his kids stayed for the full trip.

I pushed back to say that we could extend the pre-wedding days with them but that I wanted our honeymoon time to be just the two of us. When they were around, it was all about them and what they wanted. This was our day.

Hours of talking, and we were not only no longer engaged but no longer a couple. I didn't understand why even our actual marriage had to center around them. Every time he left me and was around anyone else, he would change plans that were meant for the two of us. I saw this in other things as well with his work and friends. Like he was a chameleon and would blend with the opinions of whomever he was with. I felt like whatever we decided would change the moment he spoke with anyone else. I really felt like this relationship wasn't about us but about his world and how I was to fit into it.

It felt like torture living so close to him but not being with him. Whenever the longing would come at me hard, I would remember how he changed and I couldn't count on him. My heart was broken. I looked at all the notes and websites and photos from the planning I had done and felt not only the loss of 'us' but I had also gotten so excited for this dream trip. I was so embarrassed to tell my family and friends again that we were not getting married.

Holding the spreadsheet of the costs and the half that I was paying, ready to throw it away, I slid to the floor, looking at it a little differently now. If I moved a couple of things around, I could still go to Hawaii. So I started planning. I dreamed of going but never thought I could on my own. I had never vacationed alone, but the things I had planned for the two of us I would happily do alone to experience them. I'd rather be in Hawaii heartbroken than here. Excitement replaced defeat, and I put together the flights, hotel, and activities for my trip.

I got so excited and reached out to Byron to tell him, but he didn't answer, so I called Claire. I told her I was coming over to tell her my news. Her children were there waiting to hear the news too. I adored them and appreciated their excitement for me. I broke the news about the engagement being off again but then dropped a stack of papers explaining that I was taking myself to Hawaii and the things I was going to do there.

Initially, Claire said to wait a week and Rob would probably change his mind, but my enthusiasm seemed to capture her. She told me to stay right there and ran downstairs. I was showing pictures to my nieces and nephews when Claire came back up. She was shouting that she was coming with me!

We booked everything that night. I couldn't believe that we were going. We were leaving in a couple of weeks, and all my time was spent dreaming and planning the days, packing, and re-packing. My heart felt shredded, but the distraction was so welcome.

We planned Waikiki Beach and Hanauma Bay, snorkeling, surfing, and skydiving at North Shore! Was I crazy? Yes, and it felt amazing! Days later, Rob reached out with a lame excuse that he needed to pick something up at my place. I made sure I wasn't there, which seemed to surprise both of us. He would text occasionally, and I had no problem this time ignoring him.

***

Hawaii was everything and more than I dreamed of. I had reservations about this much alone time with Claire, but it was perfect! Our hotel was on Waikiki Beach, so we were barefoot in the sand all the time. We watched every sunset and sunrise. Double rainbows over the island, drives through the rainforest, and amazing hikes to waterfalls. We rented surfboards and floated out soaking in the palm tree-lined beachfront and even rode in a couple of waves.

Hanauma Bay was probably my favorite with the most colorful fish I swore were fake. It looked like someone took the brightest color play-doh and wrapped them. And the sea turtles! We got to swim alongside a sea turtle feasting on coral. Laying under the shade of dreamy palm trees and watching luaus.

Rob texted while we were finishing lunch halfway through our trip, "Hey beautiful, I miss you." I don't know what came over me, but I took a selfie under the shade of palm trees with the sparkling water behind me and sent it. He immediately FaceTime me, and I picked it up. Claire was trying to pull my attention to say no, but I was so happy and squinted into my phone. He had no idea I was in Hawaii and probably as surprised as I was that I went without him. He kept texting, and I kept sending him island photos.

You won't be surprised to hear that we got back together when I returned. I learned that his kids and friends didn't know we had gotten back together this time. I kind of liked it this way. I didn't have to deal with his family. Once we were at the gym, though, his older daughters saw us, and Rob was running to meet them. They looked so confused, and although I couldn't hear what Rob was telling them, their unkind glances toward me let me know that they were not happy. Although I hoped for something different, I preferred who Rob was away from them.

I didn't know what 'together' looked like anymore, but I knew he was the one for me since we couldn't stay away from each other and decided I would take it anyway I could. We even went touring reception halls together, talking about the big wedding he wanted. He told me the style of dress he wanted me in. We weren't engaged but were planning the venue and menu. We even looked at homes. He liked the appearance of having a lot of money and would look at homes well outside of my budget and desired size. He wanted a large home with many rooms for his kids, even though they weren't with him much.

As it was expected that I would pay half, I tried many times to tell him that he should cover the extra space that he wanted for his kids, or I could never swing the high price. I couldn't help feeling like when they would be there, I wouldn't have my own home to retreat to and thought of the closets and where I could hide.

We got into conversations where I would confront him about money. He was showering his kids and even his ex with money, but all our plans were about him needing to take out a loan. I told him that we need to stay within our means, and he needed to break his ex of being able to call him asking for more money. He had already bought her house, her car, the kids' cars, the kids' phones, all the kids' activities, and she had a healthy stipend where she wasn't even working. Rob lived in a rental with not much. He just wanted his kids to appear to be rich. I found out he was still listed as the owner of the house she was living in.

He really didn't like me talking about these things, but we were talking about getting married! He wanted a grand wedding and believed his client's gifts would more than cover it, so he only needed the loan initially. This was absurd to me and we fought. He wanted to end the conversation and be in control of how money was handled. My financial business was mine, and his was his.

This time, we broke up for months. It felt like this was it, as we had never been apart this long, and the reality of what separated us was seemingly too great. I heard plenty through the grapevine that his ex was happy. I knew she had been driving wedges between her kids and me and had finally won.

TWENTY FIVE

At two and a half years from meeting Rob, and so much mental anguish of the heart, my doorbell rang. I answered it, and Rob was standing at the door, the sun setting behind him. Neither of us said anything for what seemed like forever. My heart fluttered so heavily in my chest to see him again, and I knew no love had been lost and had only grown for him. I had never felt that before.

A single tear betrayed me and fell quickly down my face. In a fluid step, Rob had me wrapped in his arms. He just held me there in the doorway, squeezing me close. I was in complete surrender, and without any words, he knew this.

He whispered in my ear that he would like to talk and asked if we could go for a walk. I excused myself to get my shoes, going to my room to wipe my face and nervously took a look at myself in the mirror. I so wanted to be with him. I was happy he was there and to hear what he had to say. Trying to appear a little distant and to hide my longing, we walked out the door. Some small talk and then some flirting before I flatly asked why he came.

He started with an apology for not prioritizing us over his kids and for telling his ex things about me that should have been private between us. He admitted that she became obsessed with me. He said he has never loved anyone like he loves me and his feelings were so strong and he needed me. That he knew he didn't treat me right and wanted to tell me everything, to come clean and see if I would ever want him again. He didn't look at me as we walked and he said these things.

He had me when I opened the door, but I was to learn the depth of what he meant when he said he wanted to tell me everything. I slid my hand in his and said yes. That night would prove to be a scar on my heart that is still here today.

We went up to my guest room, and he didn't want me to look at him while he confessed things neither of us wanted to hear. The lights stayed off, and only the moonlight dimly lit the room. He started off saying that my knowing there was something going on between him and his ex was right. That he knew if he let on before, he would lose me, so he wanted to manage it himself.

He didn't know how I knew, but he had to lie to not lose me. She was flirty and coming on to him from the time she learned he was dating me. I was the only girl he became serious with and told her how well we fit together. She would make him dinner and text or call him regularly. She would create times to meet, saying she needed to talk about the kids. He admitted that he knew what she was doing but liked the attention.

He spoke for so long, saying things that tore me up but also were the missing pieces in our story that I knew felt off. The night before my birthday, she told him that she wanted to see where things could go for them, but he had to break it off with me now as she didn't like the idea of him spending my birthday with me. So he did. They went on a couple of secret dates, not telling their kids. He swore that the most that happened between them was holding hands. After they spent the holidays together like a family, he broke things off, saying that he just didn't love her and it wasn't working.

That matched up with the time he broke up with me and got back with me. Not a beat missed. He knew I would be there if he wanted me back as long as I didn't know what he was doing.

He also shared that he dated other girls doing the same thing, where he would meet someone and break up to go on a date with them and then come back to me. He said he was remorseful as they were never anything he ended up wanting and how he would take them to really nice places, knowing they were accustomed to more than I ever had.

When he finally stopped talking, I said, "So you were cheating on me, realized now that I am what you want and want me back?" He got really upset, insisting that he never cheated because he broke up with me before dating any of them. I said, "That is cheating!" He stood to leave but stopped himself and said that he knew he didn't deserve to be trusted and offered me his phone to see the conversations he had had. I took the phone and started scrolling through the text messages with his ex. Middle-of-the-night long conversations. Scrolled to just before my birthday. Around our engagements. I was sick to my stomach and wanted to cry, to yell... but I couldn't stop reading.

These were books of conversations, and so many things started filling in the gaps of our on-again/off-again relationship. He reached out at one point, trying to take back his phone, but I pulled away. He wasn't just a liar; he was an expert at deception. His ex was even more terrible to me than I imagined. There was a text to his ex about my tax bracket and how I never had much, to which she made fun of me. I got to see what a horrible person she was. Even when she knew we were engaged, she relentlessly flirted and sent pictures.

I finally handed him back the phone, still facing the window with him behind me. He stood there waiting for me to say something, but I didn't have words. The torrential storm inside me held my tongue tightly.

He spoke softly and said he was so sorry again and that he understood if I never spoke to him again and how much he loved me, begging for me to forgive him and give him another chance. He waited there. How dare he think I might jump in his arms? Eventually, he turned and said he would leave now, but I could reach out anytime. I let him leave and heard his footsteps down the stairs to the front door. When I heard the door shut, I buried my face in the pillow and cried all night.

I spent every day and night trying to forget him. My heart was shattered, and I didn't know how to go on. I went through the motions each day required of me but spent the rest of the time in darkness alone. I hated that I fell in love with him before I knew what he did. It would be so easy to forget him if he came clean the many times I asked very direct questions about what he was doing. I would have walked away without a second thought.

They made such a fool of me. It wasn't like he just omitted the truth - I asked him point-blank many times, and his slick tongue lied, putting this on me, making me think I was a jealous girl. I never felt jealous of her. She was an ugly person from the inside out. I thought she was manipulative, but finding out they both were.

Through the years dating him, I had listened to the Cranberries song "Linger" many times. Now I had it on repeat. It seemed to describe our relation-ship. His lies and my staying anyway. How stupid I was. Time showed me that love is an addiction. Even when it's bad for you, you're so desperate for more. Why wasn't I able to stop feeling love for him? Was he as good as it gets for me? I was trying so hard but couldn't function without thinking of him.

Flowers with sweet notes were left on my doorstep, and text messages of apologies and pro-fessed love kept coming. "Good morning Sunshine" texts every day. My heart yearned for the dreams I had created over these years with him. I wondered if I was to forgive him, that we could have what I always wanted. I started to reason that maybe he wasn't sure before, but he seems sure now. So I asked him to come over.

He was excited and insisting that he would make everything right and would never hurt me again. He apologized that he was confused, but he wasn't confused now, believing that he was trying to figure things out and protecting me from that. Wrapping me in his arms, I felt so hopeful.

Although things were wonderful again with us, maybe even better than before, his kids, ex, and others acted in ways that I could tell were not welcoming. They didn't understand why he was with me, and I learned some very hard ways that he didn't clear things up with anyone else. They were looking at me as playing with his heart and hurting him. I asked him to tell them the truth so they didn't see me that way and would want us together. He would insist that he would, but the time was never right.

So I waited. I imagined that once they knew it wasn't me that was playing games and hurting him, I would be welcomed and they would see how kind and loving I was and how Rob was lucky to have me. He even talked about how one day, when I am ready, we could get married in the beautiful venue we previously toured and then jet off to Hawaii for the honeymoon alone. My friends and family didn't understand why I was still with him. They would try to set me up on dates and said I deserved better. My heart was locked on Rob.

The wars in my mind I experienced became more than I could bear. I felt anxious and untrusting; fearful and increasingly angry; resentful and wanting to leave but wanting more to be with him. I would have panic attacks at the war inside my heart and mind.

Time went on and on, but he never set anything straight. I told him that was needed for us, or I would never be welcomed. He would only say that everyone expects us to be together, and no one is treating me otherwise. This wasn't true. His family was cold and distant. Something in me was creating space because of this. His words said he loved me, but his reputation was more important. Each time we were together, I would see a break in the sunshine of our love, questioning his care for me.

He was good at deflecting some of these issues on his ex or kids but never himself. He had a way of talking to me and making me feel safe for the moment but never changing the narrative. Maybe this was why he was so good at his sales job.

I struggled to push down the persistent thoughts that love shouldn't hurt like this. That maybe I didn't deserve a love that I could trust; those were fairytales. I also had such strong feelings of not wanting to lose this. Him.

We continued to date, and he continued to talk about marriage. I was having moments of feeling like there had to be something better for me but still loved him. All around me, people were telling me to leave him, but I persisted. The only time we spent now was without his family, and I no longer desired to try to mend that part of his life.

I wrestled with my thoughts as they pushed and pulled me in different directions. I felt like I was losing my mind. His words and actions contradicted each other, and I could see that wasn't going to change. He would never put his reputation on the line for us. I waited for so many years to be chosen and finally settled on something that wasn't what I wanted but the only thing that I could handle. Trying to control what I could to calm the storm in my heart. I decided to tell him that I would never talk about marriage with him again but liked our relationship as it was. He could have his two lives.

Now I am not waiting for him to undo the damage he created. I don't have to be a part of that side of him, and I got to have the part of him that I was in love with.

I finally felt as much peace as I thought would be possible and tried not to care what he did or what was said about me when he was away. It was such a release of pressure that I felt now. The hurt was there, and I battled it often - looking like panic attacks at times.

We decided to take a trip to Cancun, and he still talked about getting married constantly. I thought I was direct before, but I made a point to gently take his face in my hands and tell him again that I love him but will never talk about marriage with him again since he insisted on keeping his friends and family believing that I hurt him and was unfaithful. I came to believe he lacked integrity and didn't trust what he would do when I wasn't around. He just smiled and kissed me.

TWENTY SIX

Jessica had responded to an outreach, and Trafton was coming to visit more. Jessica and Trafton even coordinated a joint visit where they asked if I would consider moving back to Colorado. If I did, so would Trafton, who was living in Seattle. Within that same breath, I was making plans to move. I never asked Rob, but I told him it was happening. I thought our relationship could continue long distance if he wanted, but I had to go. He said he didn't want to lose me and he could do this while his kids were still at home. He said he could see having homes in both states.

Within a couple of months, I was in my car following Rob, who was driving the moving van. My kids welcomed him as we unpacked into my new home. I was having breaks in my life where Rob wasn't there. I even started feeling resentments toward him and how he let others talk about me and treat me. Maybe I was allowing myself to feel these things because my life was blossoming outside of him.

Over time, Rob started pushing more for marriage again, and I challenged his reasons. It was his reputation and how he could explain coming to see me. He broke up with me over text one time out of the blue, and within a couple of days, was back like nothing had happened. I asked who he dated since I knew he would break up to see other people before. He was quiet for a moment and then pushed back that it was because I wouldn't talk about marriage, so it was my fault.

  We had now been together for five and a half years, and although I didn't want to see life without him, I definitely didn't like what married life with him would be. He even made it clear that being married would financially benefit him, as clients trust him more when they know he is married. If we did it by the end of the year, it would also be a tax break. How romantic!

  Thoughts would come to my mind and heart about how he loved me on his arm and how the things I did for him and the way I was always saying sweet things made him happy and stroked his ego. He loved what my presence in his life gave him. How I made him feel with constant compliments and all my attention. He was both of our priority. Instead of him thinking, "Wow, what a wonderful woman I found," I now believe he was thinking, "Look how amazing I am that she does these things for me."

  During this time, I learned things in bits and pieces but found out that with his ex not working or working a part-time job at minimum wage, the cost of university for his kids was next to nothing. They only claimed her income, which allowed them to receive modified tuition. Although he could easily pay, and she could work, they took a program designed to help low-income families to have the same opportunities. This was one of many. Loopholes. Lack of integrity. I questioned my own morals at this though and wondered if I would do the same. I would give anything for my children to have the chance his kids had.

I was excited to see him, but after a short amount of time, I was ready for him to leave. Months of getting together, breaking up, fighting, making up, and finally, we were just done. For real this time. Slowly as love faded, clarity was found. Oh, the pain of the heart that would linger though. Although I often ached for him, I could see that the only thing we always had in common was our mutual love for him.

I threw myself into my kids and their lives and was so happy. Lots of time with Trafton and Jessica, which filled my heart. I had to put myself in front of Ren, but when I did, he was kind and loving. He never reached out on his own, but I thought I understood why.

I tried dating a little but knew my heart was still with Rob. I wasn't ready and really didn't trust myself anymore. I didn't trust my own judgement and most of all, I could see that when I was in love, I lost who I was and allowed things to happen that I never would outside of the love-haze. I could see that the anxiety and restless mind I had when Rob was part of my life was now gone.

Life was wonderful with the kids and their worlds that I tried so hard to be a part of. All my family outside of my children were out of state. I found myself living for the time I had with the kids and built up my home in anticipation of them all gathering near.

Since they were all grown and had their own homes, most of the time I was alone. I didn't have any friends or co-workers nearby, and the few dates I went on left me feeling more lonely than before. I didn't know how to trust anyone. I felt confident that there are wonderful men with integrity but feared it would take years to really know, and with my heart involved, my brain seemed to be mush.

I didn't need to sign up for responsibilities and relationships that took far more than they gave. I self-isolated as the only way I knew not to be in the line of hurting anymore. Whether I created this or others did, this seemed to be the only sure way to keep it out. The less people I was around, the less chaotic my life was.

Inner work became my pastime. I noted patterns of chasing and begging for people to be in my life. Why do I stay when things feel impossible? At every step, I remembered when my intuition was screaming at me. Why is it so hard to act on it? I have tried before but need to heal the past to make sure my future doesn't bring any of the same forward.

Making this a daily practice, I started a journal to note of what I'm learning so I can look back and hope to see remarkable progress. I pulled out my old university class audio recordings and books from Jack

Kornfield and Dan Siegel, who train therapists in the practice of mindful meditation.

Outside of my children, I will walk away from anyone and anything that brings those feelings back, especially when I feel the intuitive warning. I talk big but have fallen short when love is near. I cannot fail me again. Relationships have taken so much, often without me even noticing what I needed. I'm weary of quietly shaping myself to fit the spaces others had me hold.

God isn't answering or fixing things. Family conditionally loves me. The men I choose lack integrity, with me at least. Am I training others how to treat me? Do I agree that I don't deserve more? I look at the broken pieces of my life and want to create a different me and a different life. I want a do-over.

I search. Searching for meaning, answers, and belonging in this new landscape. I've moved again, am working from home, and have left my church. Many of the major ways to find new connections. What a perfect place to start over, right?

I've come to see that people tend to move in circles that feel familiar and safe. Years of shared history and routines have formed strong bonds, leaving little room for someone new to slip in. As adults, we are busy, guarded, and more aware of the cost to let someone close. Familiarity becomes comfort, and comfort becomes a boundary. These circles are often already established and closed. Add to this the political climate and those who feel a single woman is a threat.

The place I now live has some very strong and large circles. I don't fit in either the close military family or the mega church community. It's not that we don't still have plenty in common, but polite introductions become a quiet sorting where I'm filtered out.

I have always believed in God, but the things I saw, heard, and experienced created more questions than answers. I would hear people saying that God saved them when others around them died. Or that God blessed them. So was he punishing others? Torture and torment on some with ease and privilege for others?

It was easy to find people sharing their stories and experiences online, and their perspectives helped to challenge mine. I knew the things I went through were nothing compared to what others had faced. There were also many who seemed to have a privileged and easier life from the beginning. I really struggled to understand the massive unfairness.

I looked at my own life and recall begging to God for help, answers, miracles - but nothing came. I always wanted to be a mom but also felt that I completely failed. Bathing in regret for all my choices, but other than feeling bad, it didn't change anything. Outside of checking out of living, I didn't feel confident in the future being better. I created distance with my extended family and moved so many times that I have found myself alone. Protected, but alone. My children and now grandchildren are all that feels safe in this world.

I heard a saying that we create our experience and wondered if this is true. I certainly wouldn't have created the things that I went through on purpose. Everyone seemed to have the answers but me. I felt sure of my purpose when the kids were young and needed me. Now what?

As a child, I was taught that we are given challenges and must endure them. That God wouldn't give more than we could handle. That my purpose was to find a partner, have children, and serve others. That this life is a test and pass or fail, it will determine my place for eternity.

With circumstances and opportunities being so broadly different among people and cultures, this never sat well with me. So we have this one shot that determines all of eternity? Whatever belief or religion you were born into was the only right one or right way? We can't all be right, but people seem so sure in their beliefs. Why is there so much confusion?

I learned about energy and vibration and how what we think and believe will draw more of the same to us. I think it would be easier for someone to vibrate hope and joy if that has been their experience. For those who had pain, hunger, and fear, it would be harder to believe in something better. If what we believe brings more of the same, this just feeds into the unfairness.

After the divorce, I was hopeful that blessings would come and the challenges would lessen. Like I had to suffer and my reward would come as a result. When I met Rob, I thought that this was my earned blessing and a chance at a great relationship. That the rough road led me to him. With the feelings of love now on a shoestring, I felt instead that I was used for what I offered, and his love, too, was conditional. Am I creating this?

I wondered if God sees me. If maybe all the things that have happened were because I was less than from the beginning, like some have said. My faith in God and others was being challenged, and I feel a lack of direction. I feel that I am on my own and don't trust that anyone cares for me. It seems that everything is conditioned on what I can offer, or I have no value.

I pull away from people who profess to have the answers. Especially those who claim to be called of God and want to advise me - or against God. Learning of the financial corruption in churches and people who would only circle themselves around those similar to them while pointing their judging fingers at everyone outside of their belief system. Us-verses-them. I remember thinking I had the answers too, based on my past I knew what I thought was good and bad. Right and wrong. Time has taught me that I didn't have any answers and it felt like my best would never be good enough.

When I look around, I struggle to see love. Everyone seems out for themselves or certain it is their duty to convert, correct, or convince. Religion and politics sit at the center of this divide. Two of the most divisive forces, drawing lines where bridges might have been. Love becomes conditional, offered to those who mirror the same beliefs, the same language, the same loyalties.

Differences are treated as danger. We speak louder, listen less, and tighten the circle we move in.

We create our experience based on the thoughts we have, the feelings we carry and the actions we choose.

The emotion we tie to an event is what makes an experience unforgettable.

The more intense the feeling, the more deeply it imprints in the mind.

Strong emotional events tend to stay with us, and we often carry those feelings long after the moment has passed.

Part of healing is learning how to shorten that emotional echo so that the past stops controlling the present and future.

PART TWO
MIND

"Change your thoughts and you change your world"
-Norman Vincent Peale

TWENTY SEVEN

What I create from here and how I respond will shape what comes next. Kindness and love will be my guide. If experiences can be created from my thoughts, which led to my actions and the energy I emit that is felt by others, a new beginning starts deep within me.

I open myself to different opinions, research, and books, soaking up stories people share. Feeling especially inspired by those who were kind when kindness was not shown to them. It seemed like those hurt the most either hurt others or were the most loving. What made a person go one way or the other? These were the things that mattered to me. Who I become through the easy and hard is what is important.

I am grateful for the convenience found online to access almost anything. That can be a trap too, to consume and waste hours, but I was determined to feel inspired and fill my mind with messages of hope. I have always had vivid dreams that are mostly negative. If I felt lonely and unloved while awake, my dreams would amplify that feeling and by the time my alarm went off, I was defeated even before the day began.

I recognize that what I listen to, watch, or hear carries into my dreams. I may not have control over work and traffic, but what I allow in my home and on my radio and tv are within my abilities to choose.

While awake, it is easier to reason with and distract from negative thoughts. I was practicing meditations to reprogram what I hold onto but still found the nights and mornings to be a battle. I chose to take some time each evening to find something to watch or listen to before sleep and saved something to listen to while I got ready the next morning. Being purposeful to start and end each day on a note that would point me in the direction I wanted my life to go.

"The Boy Who Harnessed the Wind" about William Kamkwamba. "Mully" about Charles Mully, "I Am" by Tom Shadyac, "The Secret" by Rhonda Byrne, and many podcasts including popular speakers like Dr. Joe Dispenza, Jack Canfield, Jim Carrey, and Terry Crews, Denzel Washington. Filling my heart and re-programming priorities.

Seeing little glimpses of how my beliefs and experiences shaped what I did and what things were drawn to me. I could even see how I held my pain close to remind myself of what I didn't want. How I spent so much of my life vigilant in watching for the danger I was sure would come so I would be prepared to get out of its way. I thought I was learning so holding the memories was keeping me safe. Instead, this made it so I couldn't move forward. Holding relationships too long, and by doing so, I was creating from my wounds.

This is not what I wanted. I didn't know how to become this new person yet, but there were some things I did know. I knew I wanted to be kind and loving in all things. I knew that the things I listened to and the places I chose to be made this easier or harder. That my daily habits and rituals would either restrict my growth or make space for it.

No more blaming or reacting to what life gives me but actually creating something incredible. I could see that my begging and hoping came from my pain and fear. I'm learning that the energy I carry influences what I notice, what I move toward, and what naturally gravitates toward me. Hearing that we create our reality made me feel a little angry. This shined the light on my part of the story. Even in the hard places, I didn't believe I initiated. But the way I responded, the way I stayed, definitely affected how things played out.

If the universe is a magnet, then it is not rewarding or punishing. I learned about vision boards and low and high vibrations. So much information, so many techniques, and stories of others' breakthroughs were all I sought after. I noticed that if I focused on what I wanted, coupled with something I did every day (like exercise or brushing my teeth), it was easier to remember to do it regularly and concentrate longer.

I am reflecting on and seeing things differently. Maybe I stayed with Eric because of my strong emotion-driven beliefs about how my parents' divorce affected me. Maybe I stayed with Rob because I also questioned my value and wondered if he was as good as I deserved. I was waiting for them and for God to make changes. Without my beliefs, would I have stayed as long as I did? How would things have been different?

I spent a lot of time on this. Dreaming of how a different choice on my part could have a ripple effect on how it played out. I learned that parents can pass down generational fears, expectations, and beliefs that we are taught from infancy. We learn very early what it takes to feel loved. With the mindset we were born into with our family, culture, and surroundings, we then create confirmations and new beliefs from events that created high emotional responses. What thoughts are really mine and what was ingrained from birth?

I pulled out paper and pen to try and list these as they were such a part of how I identified. I don't want to expend my energy on any kind of blame but to recognize what I am holding and choose what I want to keep. I learned that we carry a lifetime of memories inside us, and our brain relies on them more than we may realize.

Every morning, without conscious intention, I return to yesterday's version of me. The same thoughts. The same emotional responses. The same beliefs about who I am and what my life is supposed to look like. This is how the past quietly rewrites my present before the day has even begun.

I find myself outside of healthy reflection at times and ended up beating myself up so much. Trying to find inner forgiveness so that I could move forward. Several times a day I would sit and notice the thoughts that would come. I named them as they came to mind. Pain, hurt, shame... I imagined that I put them in a bubble and watched them float away. I didn't need to rehash the past. Every time I thought about it, I was back there reliving it again. This did not help me and I could see that some things just needed to be stepped over and walked away from. Who will I be without these old stories?

If I was driving or going for a walk, I would look up at the clouds and imagine placing a painful memory gently on the top and watch it slowly move across the sky away from me or change in shape and dissipate altogether. On vacation on the beach, I would imagine moments I felt angry or powerless and lay them on the sand only to watch a wave wash in and carry them off to sea. This felt gentle and a way to honor the experience or emotion but not hold onto it. I didn't have to blame or even try to understand it, just acknowledge its presence and let it pass.

I had been unconsciously choosing to hold tight to these things that hurt. If I could release them, my mind wouldn't have them for reference. A new day becomes a doorway. Intention becomes the compass.

Attention becomes the paintbrush. Hope becomes the light I walk toward. Breathe. Notice. Begin again. Every day I am alive, I get to choose and create something new.

I stopped turning on the news in the morning and kept the radio off on my drive into work. Music has a way of pulling me back into old memories. It is a real-life time traveler! I just needed to stay focused on my new mission, my new self. I didn't do this all the time but in the mornings especially to keep my intention for the day clear. It's not always easy to be with my thoughts and very hard to follow them as they jump around. The little things I do daily were changing how I was feeling in a big way. I am excited to see that I might be able to create a new narrative.

Practicing how I will act and speak. How I won't allow things outside me to stick and shake away thoughts that weren't part of my new vision. Putting things into practice was hard most of the time. I would do great, and then life would snap me back. I kept listening to guided meditations and working toward catching my thoughts. I found that once I was with family, old friends, and even co-workers, I was pulled back to their familiar version of me. I have played roles for so long and it felt different for everyone when I attempted a change in me.

I noticed that I would stay small and quiet around some people and felt silly and talkative with others. Fear was dictating this. The places and people I tried to please and be agreeable with were the places and people I felt judgment from. Why did I need their approval? I believe we are all many layers of complexity. Different people and different situations see only a sliver of what makes me me.

In the past, I would look at a situation where my emotions were strong and blame the situation or other people involved. When my children would come to me hurt, I didn't help them point the finger outward but sat with them in their feelings, inquiring why they felt sad or hurt. I knew what was lasting and important in that moment as the parent. It's easy for me to say as I didn't feel the emotional reaction they did.

Life will throw things at them that won't feel good their entire lives. People and situations come and go. Being able to identify the source of our feelings would help us cope better. If I could help my children recognize that they felt this way because they wanted to be accepted and liked, for instance, we could be having a meaningful life lesson in self-acceptance and confidence. Otherwise, it would be about mean people and how to get them back, prove them wrong, or avoid them.

Why didn't I treat myself the same? If the focus was on the outside thing that triggered the strong emotion, there would never be personal growth or the intimate look at why that thing was triggering. It can feel easier in the moment to blame the situation, but in the long run, the narrative I give it will affect me long after this moment has passed.

TWENTY EIGHT

What I think about things is what gives them meaning. If someone was cussing me out in another language, assuming I couldn't read their body language, it wouldn't affect me at all. It's the meaning I give it that hurts me. I do not have to respond; that is my choice. My mind will quickly jump in, but not always in a way that will feel good to me later when the defensiveness has calmed down. We feed off each other. I wonder how many times I played the victim when I could have supported my own growth instead. How my reaction or response greatly affects myself and anyone involved.

I replayed situations where I didn't feel good about an interaction. Taking the focus off of what someone else did and just imagining different actions taken by me and how that could have changed the exchange. What it would look and feel like if I snapped back, if I returned a glare or eye-roll, a smile, or even a hug. Some of these thoughts made me laugh as I couldn't imagine how a hug in response to meanness would be received. It certainly wouldn't be forgotten, even if in the moment it was rejected.

I don't know that I have the courage to hug people or the wherewithal in the moment, but I recognize that every person has their own struggles and perceptions. An unexpected response of any form of kindness could change the outcome. I could practice, though. Just this thought has brought me joy and imagery I can use to rehearse how to be. If I practice, the response I want to lead with, it will be at the ready and maybe even become my default reaction.

This would mean that a moment could be responded to with what was happening only in that moment. My emotional reaction is limited to this exchange only. Even if I feel irritated as a response, I can quickly turn it around and not pull from some deeply held hurt. Most often, I imagine it doesn't have anything to do with me personally, but even if it does, I want kindness as my response.

I replayed out loud who I would be and how I would speak and what I would act like. It was great at the beginning, but I easily slipped back into the familiar. This was going to take some time and intense focus. Funny how I always thought people should have it together and all figured out by a certain age, and now I see this is a lifelong lesson.

Something I did know is that I take myself too seriously unless I'm around someone I am very comfortable with. Then my sense of humor and sarcasm would come out. It felt good to laugh at myself and make others laugh. I wanted this side of me to not be tucked away anymore. I think this was another reason

I stayed with Rob. This side of me was more exposed with him than with anyone else. I am grateful that he made me feel safe that way.

Some of the notable things I heard while listening to others' journeys I wrote down on sticky notes and left them in various places throughout my house. Sprinkled little reminders that my goal isn't getting through the day but creating something bigger and more important.

A man who had his heart broken shared that some people don't want love but relief from the pain they haven't dealt with, and others just want to be admired.

Another said that our identity is fluid and it isn't fixed. It's a flow of repeated thoughts, actions, and emotional patterns. The 'me' that exists right now is simply the result of years spent practicing certain ways of being. Our need to control the environment is actually just fear.

Of all the things I was learning, gratitude was the number one shared attribute to improve thinking. Training your brain to notice and appreciate abundance. This helps us to become more optimistic, resilient, reduce depression, enhance decision-making, and problem-solving. Shifting the focus to notice the positive.

Gratitude is a thought but also a feeling. It changes how we meet the world. I've seen what negative strong feelings, or emotions, can do in my life.

Recognizing and deeply feeling the emotions of gratitude can improve our relationships.

I also need to learn to trust again. Listening to that gut feeling, trusting that the answers will come. Even if I falter, all is not lost. I worked on observing my thoughts and vividly imagining how I wanted to be instead. Previously believing that people's constant need for validation and assurance was weakness and dependency. Seeking completeness in others and not being able to be alone with oneself was where I saw many people. I had decided that self-reliance and learning to navigate challenges on my own was better.

Although there is some truth to this, my self-isolation became a way to control outcomes. Trying to find a balance between not needing others to be okay, receiving the benefits of connection, and not losing myself in the process. How do I not abandon myself when others demand more than I have to give?

I appreciate the grit that I discovered. There were times that I didn't know if I could keep going, but knew I only had myself and failing wasn't an option. If I hadn't been alone in those moments, if I thought someone would have my back, I might not have pushed through. I may never have known my own strength. Why would I insist on struggling if I didn't have to? The pleading with God to save and rescue from difficult times were desperately wanted, but I would never know who I am and what I'm capable of.

I sat with this for some time. Scribbling on a notepad times where something came up in life that I didn't like, didn't want, or didn't know how to handle. How quickly I prayed for it to be taken away from me. Even without facing anything difficult, I prayed for all the wonderful things I wanted to make life more enjoyable and easy. What would that event turn out to be if I got what I asked for when I asked for it? What would my life look like? Who would I be? Maybe I would just be an insufferable brat who demands more, never to be satisfied.

Opening my mind to challenging old thoughts and working to separate the emotion from the event, I'm feeling differently and noticing things changing around me. Noting coincidences and inspirations. I was imagining events I wanted that seemed too far-fetched for reality, but then a thought would come to mind that made me think it was possible. A thought about something I could do to make it happen.

I noticed little morsels of thoughts come to my mind, like how I believed that Rob and I had a special connection and compatibility. Maybe we were simply filling each other's unresolved issues and wounds, which would feel like compatibility because the other literally filled the spaces we hadn't healed within ourselves. I can take this lesson and learn from it, making the changes in me that are needed.

Bob Proctor talked about how our thoughts carry frequency. He mentioned that we can think of someone, and they might reach out seemingly out of nowhere. I played with this, and sometimes it really did happen! If our thoughts have this power, I wanted to make sure and send hugs to my children. Even if there is no outreach, my thoughts of love can reach them and that brings me peace.

Just because I don't understand how this works or receive instant phone calls doesn't mean it isn't happening. I want to be careful with my thoughts and make sure they align with the person I want to be.

I was tripping over events that put me in places I could grow. One of these happened at my company's Christmas party. I felt I had made my appearance, been seen by the right people, and was quickly headed for the door. There was a small gathering of women all leaning in as our HR director was talking and wiping away tears. She had taken a leave of absence, so I hadn't seen her in quite a while. I wondered what was the matter and slowed down trying to eavesdrop. She had been diagnosed with something and was so afraid as she was a single mom to a toddler. As I walked past, the women opened a space for me, so I joined in.

She was recalling the fear of leaving her daughter without a mom and was feeling worse with her treatments. Afraid this was going to kill her as she was getting weaker. She was desperately trying everything she could and was told about a technique called mental rehearsal. She shared that she would close her eyes and see herself healthy and playing with her daughter. Feeling the grass under her feet at a park and laughing. Then she would spend time mentally scanning her body from her toes to her head and circling the affected area. Sending gratitude and perfect health out like a hug.

She did this many times each day, and believed it was healing her. The tests were showing that she was improving, and she believed it was her mind that was the healer. Back now at work, as there was no sign of anything wrong, and she is so grateful. Her story had us all in tears, and we collectively hugged her in celebration.

As I drove home, I thought about this mental rehearsal technique. I remembered a handful of medical events I had faced and how, somehow, I had managed to recover from each difficult hurdle. Surviving the car accident and regaining full use of my leg. Enduring pain without needing narcotics. Living with a kidney that should have ruptured and poisoned me for a year while I was misdiagnosed. Recovering from surgery that caused so much internal bleeding I required a transfusion. And the tick bite that sent me to the hospital, unable to walk, numbness spreading through my arms and legs—the doctors confident I would be paralyzed or develop Lyme disease, yet after a week I was walking again and never tested positive.

I don't know how I made it through each of these challenges. Every time, the doctors told me I was lucky. And yet, it felt like more than luck—I felt gratitude. Gratitude for the healings I experienced, and for the body that carried me through it all. Any one of those events could have taken my life or made it so much harder.

I will add this to my practice. Me hearing her story was no accident. This was meant for my heart. No need to wait for sickness or tragedy to include mentally rehearsing health and wellness, even love. There was so much to be grateful for! Maybe my vibrations were bringing these inspirations to help me with my journey.

TWENTY NINE

Some work days drain my energy more than others. It's these times I want to do nothing but stare at a wall. I know this is a trap for me, so I tied up my shoes and walked out the door. I needed to move. I opened the Calm app, but couldn't focus, so I scrolled through some short podcasts and landed on one that was light and funny. I placed my phone in my jacket pocket, pulled my gloves on, ready to wake up my body.

I was really focused on my speed now and in a much better headspace. The podcast ended too quickly, and an advertisement was playing. I was staring at the clouds and didn't want to break the heightened state I was in. A new podcast started playing, something about abused federal funding. Ugh. I worked to get my glove off and reach into my pocket, but right as I was going to turn it off, the man said something about states' incentives to break up families. I held the phone in my hand but let it play a minute longer.

Title IV-D is what he was speaking about. Incentives for states to order child support to gain access to these federal funds. I stopped paying child support many years ago, so this didn't pertain to me at all, but there was some kind of nudge from within to listen.

He shared his experience and difficulty fighting the state and the massive amounts of money involved. How these federal programs are designed and what the states need to do to get the funding. He shared that there is almost no appeal process, almost no oversight. It was his belief that states are highly incentivized to issue child support and are profiting to the tune of trillions of dollars to states nationwide.

He continued about the child code that maximizes Title IV-D reimbursement. He fought for his case and said that most people don't have the means or time, but he was lucky he did and won. Then he said that there is another title even worse and more abused, which is Title IV-E on the foster side.

I don't know when I stopped moving, but I was frozen in place with electricity firing through my entire body. That is where this podcast ended, but I stood noticing the goosebumps covering me head to toe. Every cell in my body was on alert and focused. There was something about this that is related to our experience when the state went after Ren!

I asked aloud, "Does this have anything to do with what happened to us?" I KNEW that I was meant to hear this. This wasn't just a random thing that played. This message was here for me specifically and to get my attention. Is this what they meant by inspirations and synchronicities will come?

I ran home to learn more, grabbing my laptop and typing in "Title IV-E." Pages of information and websites were at my fingertips. This is real and publicly available information!! My gut KNEW this was directly related to the hell we went through with Ren. I just had to learn more. Could this explain why the state did what they did? Will this answer the questions I have held for all these years and the devastating pain caused?

Initially, the description of the Title sounded good. To help fund the services that families need. But I found that whenever child protective services takes a child, the state gets paid. The first bit of research showed $50k per child. Podcasts and videos of people who have experienced this, and many who filed claims against different states were coming up in my searches. One in particular was in Texas and was showing the public data of the dollar value coming in each year. They get paid for foster children and adoptive children.

I found reports of claims filed in different states where families claimed they felt targeted, finding children from working-class parents that couldn't afford a lawyer to take the child—sometimes adopt them out. These are federal funding streams in U.S. child welfare. Searches showing filings and citings for improper placement across the county, misuse and mismanagement, claims that children were wrongly removed/placed or held in foster care.

I was screaming inside. My vision seemed clearer, my focus was lasered in. Every cell was at full awareness and attention.

I looked at the requirements for the states to gain access to these federal funds and found 1. that the states are to invest in the system/programs. Maybe this is why they created their own programs that we had no choice but to use theirs. Like a layered business account where funds are just moved between entities that all benefit the same groups. 2. Staying at home would be contrary to the child's welfare. 3. Be determined unsafe to stay at home by a court. 4. Have ongoing court oversight. 5. Be in a state-licensed foster care setting or program. 6. Payments to caseworkers, administration, and training (to include court-related roles).

I'm not listing the sites as the floods of pages I visited are so numerous and repeated the same story. I am not validating any of the information either, but the things I was reading sure felt relevant in my heart. I will list a .gov site that I pulled the requirements from.

https://acf.gov/cb/fact-sheet/title-iv-e-foster-care-eligibility-reviews-fact-sheet

I'm not even claiming that this Title is inherently bad. I just know that my heart tells me it was used to financially benefit the state and their programs at the expense of my son, who they had no right to go after!

I started searching what my state was receiving and using AI to help me. It painted a picture that answered the why to the questions that rang in my head from over twenty years ago to today.

I asked AI (ChatGPT) how much in Colorado claims from the years we were involved with the state. It showed approximately $35 million - $55 million for the years I entered. Then I asked it to compare Colorado to six other states (due to the system's limitations), and the populated information hit my gut in such a way that I was simultaneously disquieted and elated at finally having a glimpse of understanding.

I continued to ask for more data to show if this number has increased or decreased over the years. AI shows its sources, so I cross-referenced too. Colorado last year was up to $200 million just for Title IV-E.

It sure looks like families breaking up financially benefits the states. Regardless of my opinion, based on the information received, I knew that this was directly related to what we were put through. Not only was I paying into the 'programs,' but the state was being given high dollars on the head of my son. How many others were faced with something similar? How many of those parents felt defeated and lost their children to the system instead of receiving help if it was in fact needed?

I cried thinking back to the confusion when we were told the state was filing charges even when the family backed away. The video that proved there was no rape or attempted rape. The 'professionals' that tried to take my son twice and used the legal system and law enforcement to support them. The financial gouging we experienced. The devastating impact on a young boy. The devastation on his siblings and torture of our family.

I don't know what to do with this information. I feel that it will be a cause I will be active in to make sure this doesn't happen to others. At least not in the dark where I felt ashamed and confused.

There is something about this that will bring answers, hopefully for Ren, but we can't be the only ones. Money breeds corruption.

THIRTY

My memories are very clear, which has come in handy, but it can also make it harder to move forward. There have been times where my children will ask about something specific from their childhood, trying to find answers for themselves. Especially around the divorce and things they were being told by Eric.

I'm so grateful that I remember the details because it was in the details that helped them make sense of a situation. Times where Trafton and Jessica would ask questions, I could put the pieces together for them. I hold these memories tight in case Ren ever opens up one day.

I feel a desire to honor my story by writing it down, but getting it out of my head and burying it. If I don't have to carry this story forward, I can create from where I am now. As long as I hold these memories, I don't know that I can ever create a new life. I choose to do this literally and physically, to bury my printed story under my favorite tree. I no longer will have to rehearse it, retell it, or relive it. Its hold on me would be laid aside. Not welcome to come with me in my present and future while I build the thoughts I want to keep and let go of any suffering and stories that hold me here.

As I write, I also desire to find forgiveness in the story. Forgiving myself and others so I can emerge the person I want to be. As I write, I can see that although I kept people in my life who had hurt me, I was wearing a badge of pride thinking that it was because I had forgiven them. The truth was that I compartmentalized the person they were when they did the hurtful things and the person I needed them to be now. My dad, Mom, and Bill were in my life, but I held very strong boundaries that only I knew about. When I would recall the pain, I could see that forgiveness wasn't really there. Not fully.

Over the years, there have been many things in these relationships that continued new hurts and abandonment, so it wasn't that the hard things happened a long time ago; apologies were made, and now they were over. Relationships are messy. The past just fed into new hurts. We would lose contact for a while and try again a little here and a little there. Each time, feeling the relationship was more fractured and fragile.

If I take responsibility for my role in the story, then I have to change. Holding on creates a low vibration. With the learning that my vibration and energy are magnetic, I have a lot of work to do to change the narrative.

I started a new journal page for each person in my life that I wanted to focus on. I would write a short introduction on who they were to me (mother, stepfather, sibling) and a list of words I would use to describe my version of them. I tried to put myself in their shoes, looking at me, and, with a different color pen, write words I thought they would use to describe me. Then I would highlight the words that may not be true. This was tough, but I could see how my colored lens of them changed how I described them and how I treated them even today. I assumed it worked the other way around too. I didn't like the words describing me and didn't believe them to be true.

    I played around with many things like this to challenge my mind's view. Wondering what it would be like to meet them today with no past history. Wow, that really made me look at them so differently. I was seeing progress but also frustrated that it was slow and so easy to slip back. I didn't know anyone on this journey in my own life to talk to about it.

    I tried to use the online resources when I could and enjoyed the information, but it just wasn't consistent enough. Day-to-day life left me drained of the energy needed to make the impact I was seeking. After making only baby steps forward, I decided that I wanted to be surrounded by others also looking for this growth in a setting where we were immersed in learning and supporting each other.

    Online, I found that there were many retreats and conferences that bring groups together that might really help. These required time off, travel, and substantial costs, though, and there were so many. Where would I even begin? These were all over the world! Wellness, spiritual, yoga, silence, couples, meditative, medicinal, culinary, detox, wilderness, Ayurveda...

Japan, India, Sri Lanka, Bali, Spain, Mexico, everywhere, including my own city. I spent weeks looking into these enticing vacations sprinkled with some form of personal growth. The thought of a vacation really captured me, and it was all starting to feel like I was just looking at travel agency websites. Incredible resorts with too many package options and shared rooms offering discounts.

Overwhelmed and discouraged, I slowly let the idea fade away. In every meditation, though, something would be said about focusing on what you want. I don't know if that was always there, but I sure was noticing it more. I admit that I loved the idea of learning coupled with the feeling of being on vacation. Maybe those far-away retreat websites put ideas in my mind that a local class-like setting now seemed too boring.

On an otherwise ordinary Thursday at work, I was on the phone talking with a client in Florida, and I mentioned I wanted to come out sometime to see the sea turtles hatch. She was sending photos of her family's many experiences, and it was like a mini-vacation for me. I get excited thinking about these things, and after work, I went online to see the best months to go out. The results from my keyword search showed a hotel that monitors the nesting activity, and they offer turtle walks. Oh, I love this! I followed the link inside the hotel's website and pulled up their event calendar. You know, I do believe in freak happenings, fate, destiny, serendipity...

This hotel was hosting a conference coming in a couple of months that continued to build off what I had been working on! Not only could I afford it, but it would be during the hatching season! I started looking at flights and hotels and my budget. It would take a lot, but I made arrangements and purchased tickets.

I imagined walking along the beach at sunrise and sunset while the information I learned settled in my heart. The series was mind, body, and spirit. I missed the first one on the mind, so I sought out all the information available on the topic so I'd be prepared to add to my journey. Feeling both nervous and excited. Funny how they feel the same.

Our thoughts shape perception. Each thought acts as a filter on reality, influencing emotions, guiding behavior, shaping identity, and even affecting physical health. Thoughts create possibilities.

They are the lens through which we experience life, the engine driving our actions, and the sculptor of our sense of self and well-being. Becoming aware of them gives us the power to steer the mind, rather than be steered by it.

Preparation, excitement, and nervousness occupied me the week before leaving. Making sure work was covered, my flight and hotel were secured. I knew I overpacked but wanted to be prepared to dress up or down based on what others were wearing.

I had never done anything like this and felt the anticipation of meeting others who were seeking the same growth. I had so much I was hoping to learn but also felt the stress of social anxiety, being surrounded day after day. I had become so isolated; this would be a big change.

I needed to settle my mind tonight. Turning off the lights and letting my headphones carry me, I listened to this guided meditation.

"Find a comfortable position, lying down on your back. Let your arms rest gently by your sides. Close your eyes, and take a deep, slow breath in... and exhale fully. Allow your body to begin to soften. Notice the weight of your body pressing into the mattress. Feel your feet, legs, hips, back, and shoulders gently sinking, releasing tension with each exhale.

Bring your attention to your breath. Notice it flowing in and out, steady, calm, natural. If thoughts arise, simply notice them, and let them drift away—like clouds floating across the sky. You don't need to hold onto them.

Now, imagine a soft, warm light at the top of your head. With each exhale, this light flows down through your body, releasing tension and clearing your mind. Your forehead relaxes, your jaw softens, your shoulders drop. The light continues down your arms, your chest, your belly... all the way to your toes, carrying away any lingering thoughts, worries, or stress.

With each breath, you feel lighter, calmer, more at peace. Your mind becomes quiet, your body ready to rest. Know that it's safe to let go, to release the day, and to sink into sleep.

Take three slow, deep breaths... and with the last exhale, let your body completely surrender to rest. Sleep comes easily now.

Goodnight."

***

It's the morning of the conference, and I'm up early. I laid out my prettiest casual dress that was comfortable with pockets and made sure to bring a sweater and wore cute tennis shoes. I had a new notepad and the folder they gave me at check-in with the schedule. I had already highlighted things I was afraid to miss out on. There was a buzz in the entry of the hotel waiting for the shuttles. The conference offered four hotels to choose from, and seeing this many people here made me anxious, I mean excited, for the crowd this event had attracted.

The shuttle pulled up in front of a beautiful resort, and we were directed to sign in and get a name badge with a lanyard. Open doors led to a ballroom set up for breakfast. There was excited energy coming from everyone filling the space. Many large tables filled the vast room with signs directing people by the first letter in their name. I gathered a plate of food and weaved my way to the tables lettered 'T' finding a spot that faced the front or stage area.

Trying not to be obvious, I was watching others and knew they were all doing the same. Jealous of those who didn't come alone and looking at clothing to assure I made the right choice, I was ready to pivot tomorrow if needed. Realizing how silly it was that I thought it mattered, I laughed at myself. The range from dressy to professional to extremely comfortable was seen throughout the fast-filling room.

Tables filled quickly with lots of introductions and where-are-you-froms. Thank heavens for the name cards, but they were tucked under the table while we were sitting. With only three seats left open on my table, I saw this beautiful woman walking towards us, looking to see if there was a place for her. I could tell she came from privilege. From her clothes and jewelry to her hair and the way she carried herself.

Those near where she sat were warm and introducing themselves. A comforted smile showed her perfect teeth as she waved hello to everyone. There was something so familiar about her. She captured my attention as she spoke, even though she was far enough away that I couldn't hear her well. Then she laughed, and my heart leaped.

TARA!!

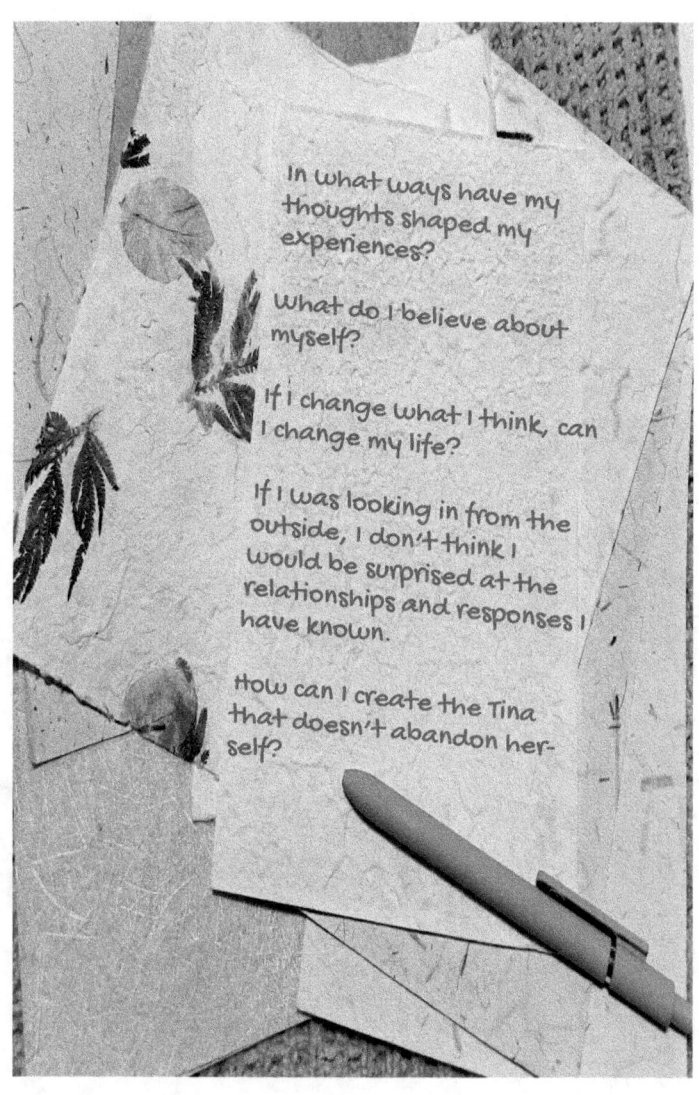

PART THREE
BODY

"We are loyal to our suffering"
        -Jack Kornfield

THIRTY ONE

My sudden realization caught the attention of the whole table as I held my nametag up and asked if her name was Tara. She looked at me with surprise and nodded yes. I knew she didn't recognize me, but I jumped out of my seat and went to her. I knelt down by her chair and told her I was Tina and we used to be friends in elementary school. Her eyes grew so large, and she pulled her sleeve up, pointing at her mole. She remembered!

Anyone within earshot was now celebrating this reunion with us. Hugs and tears and so many questions followed. We rearranged the seating so we were now next to each other. I just couldn't believe it! All these years and so far from home. The large, active room seemed muted, and it felt like it was just the two of us sharing updates and stories of our lives.

Before long, plates were being removed from the tables, and the lighting changed. Music started to play, and we knew the conference was beginning. We made promises to stay together as she held my hand, and we focused on the stage.

Our host walked to the microphone with much applause. There was excitement in the air and so much energy. I expected some formal welcome and introduction for the conference, but he just stood there until the room finally went quiet. When he started speaking, I quickly pulled out my notepad and pen.

"The body is not separate from the mind, nor is it disconnected from spirit. It is the place where both become real. Thought passes through the nervous system before it ever becomes lived experience. Meaning, too, must be carried by the body before it can be integrated. This is why insight alone does not create change. The body must be included.

Much of human behavior is not chosen in the moment. It is recalled. The body responds based on what it has learned to expect. Posture, breath, tone, emotional reflex—these are not habits of personality, but imprints of experience. When an experience overwhelms the system, the body adapts. It tightens, braces, withdraws, mobilizes. These adaptations are intelligent. They are the body's way of ensuring survival. But what once protected can later confine.

The nervous system prioritizes safety. If a past experience felt threatening, the body remains prepared for its return. Memories are not stored as stories alone, but as sensation, chemistry, and impulse. This is why the past can intrude on the present without warning. A familiar tone. A subtle look. A smell. A shift in the environment. The body responds before the mind can evaluate. Heart rate changes. Breath shortens. Emotion surges. The experience is not remembered—it is reactivated.

Thought and emotion then reinforce one another. The mind searches for explanation. The body supplies sensation. A loop is formed. Over time, this loop becomes identity. "This is just how I am." But it is not who we are—it is what the body learned. Change becomes difficult not because we lack will, but because the body prefers the familiar. Familiar states, even painful ones, offer predictability. The unknown does not. When a person attempts to think differently, the body often resists. Anxiety arises. Doubt speaks. Old narratives return. Not as truth, but as protection. The body is asking, "Is this safe?" not "Is this true?"

In the Mind–Body–Spirit framework, the body is the intermediary. The mind can imagine. The spirit can provide meaning. But the body decides whether either can be lived. Healing, then, is not about forcing the body to change. It is about teaching it safety. Through intentional presence, reduced stimulation, and conscious rehearsal, the nervous system can be introduced to new states.

Stillness slows the system. Awareness interrupts old patterns. Emotion practiced internally becomes familiar. The body does not distinguish between what is happening externally and what is experienced vividly within. Repeated emotional states—whether remembered or imagined—become learned expectations. This is how the future is embodied before it arrives. Rather than waiting for circumstances to change before feeling different, we allow the body to experience regulation first.

The body learns that safety, openness, and choice are available now. As the body settles, the mind gains clarity. As the body feels safe, the spirit gains expression. Old emotional charges begin to release. Memory loses its grip. The past becomes information, not instruction. In this way, wisdom is formed—memory without activation, experience without re-enactment.

The work of the body is not to erase the past, but to free the present. Because trauma is not stored in thought alone, and healing is not achieved by insight alone. The body remembers. And the body can learn something new.

Please find a position that feels supportive for your body. Allow your spine to be comfortable. If it feels safe to do so, gently close your eyes or soften your gaze, letting your vision rest without focus. There is nothing to fix, nothing to achieve, and nowhere else you need to be. Let your attention move to the points of contact between your body and the surface beneath you. Notice where you are supported. Allow the weight of your body to be held. Take a slow breath in through the nose...and a gentle breath out through the mouth. No need to change the breath—simply notice it.

As you continue breathing, begin to observe the natural rhythm of your body. The rise and fall.

The subtle movement beneath the skin. Let the mind know it does not need to lead right now. The body can take over.

If thoughts appear, that is okay. Thoughts are a normal function of the mind. Rather than following them, acknowledge them and allow them to pass through, returning your attention to sensation.

Bring awareness to your nervous system. Notice whether your body feels alert, heavy, restless, or calm. There is no correct state. This is simply information. Silently, you might say to yourself: This is what my system feels like right now. Allow the shoulders to soften. Let the jaw unclench. If there is tension, see if it can be met with curiosity rather than effort. Now gently bring attention to the center of the chest. Notice any sensations here—warmth, tightness, openness, or nothing at all.

Emotions often speak through the body before they form words. There is no need to label or analyze. Simply notice. If an emotion is present, see if you can allow it to exist without changing it. Let it have space. Let it move at its own pace. Now allow your awareness to widen. Notice sensations throughout the body—the belly, the back, the legs, the hands, the face. The body carries memory not as stories, but as sensation. If a memory or image arises, you do not need to follow it.

Notice where the body responds. Perhaps a tightening, a warmth, a subtle shift. Stay with sensation. Gently remind yourself: I am here now. This moment is different from the past. Bring attention back to the breath. With each inhale, imagine creating a little more space inside the body. With each exhale, imagine the body settling, as if it is being reassured.

If at any point this feels like too much, you can return to the sensation of contact—feet on the floor, back against the chair, the support beneath you. Now begin to sense the body as a whole. Not separate parts, but one connected field of experience. Notice the subtle sense of aliveness within. Silently, you might ask: What does my body need right now to feel a little more at ease? There is no need to answer. Just notice what arises.

Rest here for a few moments.

As we begin to close, bring awareness back to the room around you. Notice sounds, temperature, the presence of others. You are not alone in this experience. Gently invite movement back into the body—wiggling fingers or toes, stretching if it feels good.

When you're ready, slowly open your eyes or lift your gaze. Take a final breath in...and let it out. Carry this sense of awareness with you. The body has been listening. Welcome back. Take a moment to notice how you feel now—not in your thoughts, but in your body. Perhaps there is a little more space, a little more quiet, a little more presence. What we just did was not a pause from the work. It is the work. By settling the body, by listening instead of pushing, we created the conditions for something new to take root.

Insight can only land where the nervous system feels safe enough to receive it. Over these next few days, we will not be asking you to fix yourself. There is nothing broken here. Instead, we will be exploring—how the mind learns, how the body remembers, and how meaning emerges when the two are in conversation.

You may notice moments of recognition. Moments of resistance. Moments of relief. All of it is welcome. This space is not about striving or performance. It is about awareness, choice, and practice. Small shifts, repeated with intention, create profound change over time.

In the days ahead, we will gently examine the patterns that once protected you and ask whether they are still serving you now. We will learn to work with the body, rather than against it. And we will create room for new responses—not through force, but through understanding. You do not need to know where this journey will take you. You only need to stay present for the next step.

Each session will build on the last—education layered with experience, reflection paired with embodiment. Nothing here is random. Everything has a purpose. And perhaps most importantly, you are not doing this alone. Look around the room. Each person here has chosen to show up—to listen, to explore, to be honest with themselves. That shared intention creates a powerful field of safety and possibility.

As we move forward, I invite you to stay curious. Be gentle with what arises. And remember—your body is not your obstacle. It is your ally.

This is the beginning of a different kind of learning. One that includes your whole self. Welcome to the work ahead."

As he leaves the stage, a woman meeting him on the way to the microphone hugs him briefly and proceeds to provide us with the itinerary for the week.

THIRTY TWO

Tara and I both had so many questions for each other. Over the week, we talked late into the night and during every break. She was so sweet, and laughter came easily to her. She appeared confident, although she would add a small comment here or there about finding these lessons and how desperately they were needed.

I heard of her perfect family and some of the struggles they faced, but they were always close and loving. She had a large extended family that remained tight all her life and so many lifelong friends. She was supported, talented, smart, and given opportunities to pursue anything her heart desired. University was paid for and waiting for her with no pressure on what degree to choose. Maybe just the expectation that she would attend. Men stayed close to her support system in hopes of marrying her.

I envied her as I listened. This was the life I wanted. All the things I didn't have. I wondered who I would be if life didn't beat me down at every turn. She insisted on hearing about me too. There were tears at times, and she would hug me often. When I had hit all the main bullet points that brought us to today, she surprised me and said how she envied me.

She shared that while she really did have a good life, she felt a longing for more but felt selfish, feeling this made her ungrateful. A lifetime of people saying how lucky she was. She felt lost in her husband's eyes, wondering if he even knew her. He wanted this perfect life; and they had it. But perfect based on what? Society and culture? There was a narrative of what a good life looked like that she fell nicely into but she didn't know that this is what she wanted for herself. She was afraid to ask for more.

A good wife was to tend to the children and care for her home, volunteering and serving. But she felt lost and longed to venture out without them sometimes. She had interests in art and travel but the selfish kind where she didn't have to worry about what others wanted. Not be the kids' mom, ideal daughter, or his perfect wife.

That is part of what brought her here. She wanted to learn about and focus on finding Tara, separate from the other roles she played and loved. She had worked hard on her degree, but the babies came quickly, and her life never returned to where she could use it or continue to explore that side of her. She also had several miscarriages that really took a toll on her body and heart. Family, friends, and her church group always dismissed her sadness, saying how blessed she was to carry these babies and serve God in this way. That she was chosen to endure this.

Even if working outside the home wasn't frowned upon, she barely had a part-time job at the university while attending there so many years ago. It made her husband feel that he was an inadequate provider, and others felt that she wasn't satisfied being a mother when she mentioned maybe exploring options. She had to be more concerned with how they felt than by what she longed for.

Oh, how my heart could feel hers as she spoke. Through the exterior lens of perfection, I was ashamed of how I also judged her in wondering what she could possibly be unhappy with having a life I could only dream of.

We asked to move some of our classes and group sessions around so we could be together. As we progressed through the hours and days, I was so surprised that even though our life experiences were vastly different, we seemed to share the same struggles and life questions. When I reflected back on my life, I had believed that if my circumstances were different, I wouldn't find myself here looking for healing and answers.

As Tara and others from the groups would share their stories, so many of my beliefs were challenged and released. In classes, there was usually a lesson or story presented before a meditation. The meditations were both individual and group. Some were sitting in place, and others involved physical movement. I had been nervous about the group meditations as I was busy being concerned with how the others were sitting and if they seemed engaged; what sounds I could hear from other groups. I could tell that when I was too self-conscious, I couldn't relax.

Within three group sessions, though, I could recognize the difference in energy when I was finally able to let the ego go. Even with my eyes closed, I felt less alone and felt held without being touched. This was such a profound experience for me as I felt a sense of belonging that my life had been missing. I found myself in quiet tears for both joy and tenderness felt.

As we moved between the days' schedule, I was able to talk with others as they shared their experiences. One said that when she was alone, her thoughts would wander so much that she had never previously made it through a full meditation. A man agreed, sharing that the group setting made it easier for him to stay awake and focused.

Tara shared that she felt tingling, initially thinking she had lost feeling in her legs, but it was deeper than that. She also couldn't stop yawning. That made us all laugh.

A friend I had met from breakfast said that she had to open her eyes to break the image and emotion that pulled her into a hard place that she didn't want to feel. It made her body feel jumpy that she couldn't sit still and was afraid to disrupt everyone else. She wanted to get up but was finally able to relax again but refused to close her eyes.

A couple, who appeared to be married, made their way to our informal gathering, and she asked her husband how he felt. He clearly didn't like being put on the spot as we all focused on him, waiting for his answer. He commented that it was too long and the seats were uncomfortable. That he didn't know what sitting in a circle was supposed to accomplish.

Tara and I broke away as there was a two-hour break before the next session. I needed to lie down, and she needed to check in on the kids. We walked out to where the shuttles were waiting and agreed to meet back thirty minutes before so we could take a walk around the beautiful pond before going in.

I felt so exhausted and laid down, setting my alarm just in case. I can't even remember hitting the pillow, but the alarm shot me up quickly. I was so grateful for the privacy and nap. I needed that. Quickly gathering my belongings and brushing down my hair, I was happy that the shuttle had a spot for me as they were ready to leave.

Tara was waiting on the curb. Her bright smile and cheerful disposition couldn't hide the lack of crinkle in her eye. I felt so much love for her and the knowing that she was so sweet even in the face of her own exhaustion. It was an absolutely gorgeous day. The sun's rays looked like glitter on the pond as we enjoyed the scenery and fresh air.

We shared stories of our children and vacations. Joy and laughter were welcomed by the sun on our faces. We daydreamed of places we wanted to go and swore to stay in touch and take some trips together. We would be bold and try new things and share our journey, ever supporting and cheering each other on.

As we walked this path around the pond, we seemed to pick up new friends along the way. In life, it seems so hard to make friends, but here, everyone was an immediate friend. I never wanted this to end.

We headed in as our host was to speak on trauma held in the body, with lunch to follow.

"When we talk about trauma, we're not just talking about what happened. We're talking about what the body had to do to survive it. Trauma is not stored as a memory alone. It is stored as a response. In moments of overwhelm, the nervous system does exactly what it's designed to do—it prioritizes safety. This is not weakness or dysfunction. It is intelligence. The body adapts faster than the mind can understand. And when an experience feels threatening enough, those adaptations remain long after the event has passed.

This is why trauma doesn't always feel like a story we can tell. Often, it shows up as sensation—tension in the shoulders, a tight chest, a stomach that won't settle, a sudden wave of anxiety with no obvious cause. The body remembers even when the mind wants to move on. Our nervous system tracks safety. If something once felt dangerous, the body stays prepared for its return. It learns patterns and responds automatically to protect us.

Over time, these survival responses become habits. They shape how we move through the world.

We might avoid certain situations. We might stay hyper-alert. We might disconnect from sensation or emotion altogether.

None of these responses are wrong. They are strategies. The challenge arises when the body doesn't receive the signal that the danger has passed. When the nervous system stays activated, it begins to shape thoughts, beliefs, and identity. This is why insight alone is often not enough. You can understand what happened. You can know you're safe now and still feel unsafe in your body.

Healing requires working with the body. The body doesn't respond to logic; it responds to experience. When the nervous system repeatedly experiences safety, presence, and choice, it begins to update its expectations. This is why practices like mindful awareness, gentle movement, breath, and guided imagery matter. They are about teaching the body a new reference point.

Healing happens when the body is allowed to process what it once had to suppress. This work is not about reliving the past. It is about restoring regulation in the present, and this is important to say clearly: nothing is wrong with you. If your body reacts strongly, if emotions rise unexpectedly, if you feel disconnected or overwhelmed—these are not failures. They are signs of a system that learned how to survive.

Our work together is not to erase these responses but to listen to them, to understand them, and to help the body learn that it no longer has to carry this alone. The body holds trauma because it had to, and it can release it when it finally feels safe enough to do so.

The body hears everything your mind says. If you can think yourself into sickness, then thoughts can also create health. That is the foundation of everything we will explore together."

THIRTY THREE

On so many levels, this conference couldn't have come at a more perfect time. I couldn't get over that Tara was here and how much support we found in each other and all our new friends. I feel that I had been making good progress before coming here, but the strength in numbers really accelerated my growth. Already feeling anxious about leaving this place and having to return on my own again.

The way the schedules were designed, our close-knit group was separated many times into different group sessions provided. We agreed to meet up and share our notes and favorite messages daily.

The husband/wife team shared about when the familiar feels like love. That we can be drawn to familiar emotional states, like the ones we were raised in, but that doesn't mean they are healthy.

Tara shared a session that talked about social dependency and how it can lead to people-pleasing. This can make us rely on others to stabilize us emotionally. It's not an addiction to people, but we can rely on others to feel validated. Humans are wired for relationships, but when the body has learned to associate love with unpredictability or tension, calm can feel boring. Safety can feel unfamiliar, and we may unconsciously recreate relationships even if they are not good for us.

I shared the one I took the most notes on, which was about intuition and our gut feeling. How our body can process information faster than thought. It is not mystical. Goosebumps and chills are the body saying 'pay attention'. It is the capacity to recognize meaning quickly before analysis. Other terms that are often used are: hunch, a knowing without knowing why, instinct, discernment, impression, foresight, premonition, sixth sense, or clairvoyance. People can lose their trust in intuition. To be polite instead of honest, productive instead of rested, connected instead of safe.

Another friend shared that sighing, yawning, trembling, and tears are not signs of emotional weakness. This can be our body finally releasing the stored energy it didn't feel safe to experience. People can feel that this release of emotion is them losing control, but it is not. He noted that many of the men were nodding as though they especially felt this. He often feels in control during crisis, but once it is over, his body has these involuntary reactions and never understood this before now.

Topics of autopilot and health were also discussed. Autopilot repeats what is familiar. It conserves energy but often at the cost of awareness and flexibility. Our body has learned reactions, behaviors, and coping strategies. One of the most powerful places autopilot shows up is in relationships. This can show up as familiar emotional reactions like defensiveness, avoidance, and even agreeableness. We are not responding to the issue or person in front of us but what the body remembers. This can be especially harmful to our relationships.

Autopilot is doing today what it learned yesterday without checking whether those responses still make sense. Unconscious living is the enemy here - not autopilot.

A session focused on the connection between body and health taught that chronic stress keeps the body in protection mode. This impacts digestion, immunity, inflammation, and pain. Health is not just physical; it is physiological, emotional, and relational. The body cannot heal fully while it feels unsafe.

We were lucky to have such a diverse group. We could share all day together. The conversations were not pointed at a person or situation but with a goal of learning and becoming more aware of the places we can take these lessons into our lives to enrich everyone around us.

Music started to play from the ballroom with an announcement to gather for a closing ceremony for the day. Hugs and handshakes were exchanged as we filed down the hallway. I invited everyone to see the turtles hatch with me and we made the plan for that night.

***

"We are so pleased to see the connections forming and service shown to each other's growth. It is our hope that when we notice when something feels off, we can respond earlier and no longer need crisis to wake us up. Embodiment is listening and responding to the body in real time. Not perfection. Not constant calm. Just presence. As the body begins to regulate, clarity increases, relationships shift, boundaries become easier, and health responds.

We will end this day with a trauma-informed guided meditation designed for gentle release, not re-exposure. It focuses on safety, choice, and regulation, allowing the body to let go only what it is ready to release.

Begin by finding a position that feels supportive. Let your body choose what feels safest. If it feels comfortable, gently close your eyes. Or soften your gaze. Take a slow breath in through the nose... and exhale through the mouth. There is nothing you need to do. Nothing you need to fix. Your body already knows how to protect you.

Bring your attention to the places where your body is supported—the floor, the chair, the surface beneath you. Notice the weight of your body being held. Take another slow breath in...and let it go. Let the nervous system know: right now, I am safe enough. Now bring gentle awareness to your breath. Not changing it—just noticing where it moves most easily. Perhaps the chest, the belly, or the back. If thoughts arise, allow them to drift by. You don't need to follow them. Return to sensation.

Trauma is not something you need to remember. It is something the body learned to hold. Today, we are simply listening. Begin to scan your body slowly, starting at the top of your head and moving downward at your own pace. Notice any areas of tension, heaviness, or numbness. There is no need to label or analyze. Just notice. If you come across a place that feels tight or guarded, pause there gently.

Place your awareness there like a warm hand. You might silently say: Thank you for protecting me. Often, tension is held because it once had a job. You do not need to force release. Release happens when the body feels permission. Take a breath into that area—not to change it, just to include it. As you exhale, imagine creating a little more space around the sensation. Not pushing it away. Not pulling it closer. Just giving it room.

If at any point this feels too intense, return your attention to your feet on the floor or your back against the surface beneath you. You are always in control. Now imagine your body as a container. Some experiences settled deeply because there was no space to release them at the time. Today, you are not emptying the container. You are loosening the grip. Notice if the body wants to sigh, yawn, stretch, or shift. Allow it. These are natural signs of discharge.

If emotion arises, let it move like weather—no story required. No meaning necessary. Simply notice how the body responds as sensation changes. You might feel warmth, tingling, heaviness lifting, or noth-ing at all. All responses are valid. Now bring attention to your heart or center of the chest. Notice the rhythm there. Imagine sending a message inward: you don't have to hold this anymore—at least not all of it. Let the body decide what it releases. You don't need to choose. Stay here for a few breaths.

As we begin to close, bring awareness back to your whole body. Notice the space you're in. The sounds around you. Feel your feet, your hands, your support. Take one final slow breath in...and let it out. When you're ready, gently open your eyes or lift your gaze. Take your time. Healing doesn't happen by forcing the body to relive the past. It happens when the body learns it is safe enough to let go."

***

Groups were gathering and making plans for the evening. There were people who were coupling up, curious if they may be starting a love story from such a magical setting. We met on the beach behind a netted fence to watch for the turtles. Huddled with blankets around our shoulders as the sun set, burning incredible memories I will cherish as the light stretched across the water.

No activity in the sand, we sat down waiting. Around 9:30 p.m. most of the crowd had moved on. I wanted to stay, and Tara agreed. All the talking stopped, and we found such peace in seeing, hearing, and watching the waves come in and out. The moon shone bright in the night, softly illuminating the sand around us. I was thinking about how grateful I was for everything unfolding in my life, but more than that, I was feeling the gratitude. Starting with a growing warmth, pushing tears from my eyes, and lifting the corners of my mouth. I rested my head on Tara's shoulder.

With a shush from the conservation guide, it happened! Slowly at first and then just a wave of movement from the sand. The tiniest little turtles making their way to the water. A sweet reverence fell over the small group peering over the makeshift fence. Some climbing over others with their impossibly tiny flippers carrying them to the moonlit shoreline.

So happy we waited! It was pretty late, and the room I was in had two beds, so I invited her to stay over. In the dark, Tara shared that she really loved her husband but needed things to change. Her fear of even broaching the subject with him created imagined scenarios with negative outcomes each time. As I listened, I didn't know what to say to help her but dreamed that maybe if she left him, we could create a close relationship. As soon as I thought this, I realized how selfish I was being.

I asked her to tell me how they met, and she told a story of excitement and love and things I've only heard of in fairytales. She glowed in her memories and praise of how he treated her, protected her, and found great pride in his care for her and the children. He was boastful of her cooking and made sure Mother's Day was the most celebrated day of the year.

She shared photos, glowing from her phone, of their life together. I admit that I dripped in jealousy of her world but felt so genuinely happy for her. She has always been such a sweet soul and couldn't help but feel how amazing he must be to have won a tender heart like hers.

I asked about his response to her desire to use her degree or branch out, expanding her motherhood role. She spoke of some little hints here and there but never an actual conversation. I challenged her to think it out and prepare a time they could seriously discuss her feelings. He seemed to love her dearly. Maybe she was challenging their beliefs on gender roles but maybe her vulnerability would allow him to explore evolving identities without fear of judgment also.

THIRTY FOUR

Music has always been such a big part of my life but I am more intentional about what I listen to now and how it makes me feel. I had it playing in the background as I bopped around the room getting ready for the day ahead, recognizing the power to lift that music had. Feeling so much gratitude and sending lovetexts to the kids. Both Jessica and Trafton quickly responded with sunshine and heart emojis. Jessica called on FaceTime with the grandlittles to say hello. Their sweet faces and cheerful silliness filled my heart. She and I have become so close, sharing in the joy of a new generation. Plans of events and sports and dreams of creating wonderful memories danced in my head. When the call disconnected, I held the phone to my heart, holding them just a little longer.

Trafton gave me updates on his precious one and shared his exhaustion and joy along with photos of them playing together. She is totally a daddy's girl! They have no idea how much these messages mean. Ren stayed distant, but whatever he shared with his wife made me her enemy. As mean as she has been, I believe she thinks she is protecting him from me. I tried to connect with her, but her responses put me in tears, which only brought a smile to her face. I still send gifts when I can and send messages occasionally but don't attempt any other form of relationship after all these years of nothing from Ren.

I had packed up my things and was ready, especially early. Hope and excitement for life made me more ready to start each day. I set my alarm when the shuttle would come so I didn't need to think about the time and made myself comfortable, propped up by the pillows on the bed. Closing my eyes, I continued thoughts about my family. Each one. How close I was with my mom and how difficult our relationship has been. Over the years, there were many times that she and Bill would just push me out of their lives. If I tried to call, I would be hung up on. Mom once told me that it would be different if there weren't so many other children. My response cut deep, "You shouldn't have more kids than you could love". So many past wounds that kept surfacing.

As they have gotten older, we have a rhythm where I call, and sometimes they will answer. I can visit briefly but always feel a little unsure of how it will go. It works well enough. I want her in my life but within limits, as I'm sure they would agree. We are in a place now where Mom and Bill will text kind encouragements and sweet messages. I am grateful for this.

I happened to live in the same state as my dad for a couple of years and felt a sort of obligation to see him. We would go out to dinner or the movies and talk for hours about philosophy. He was incredibly smart, but I always thought it didn't help him as he couldn't apply it to create better relationships— alone after many failed marriages. The conversations were interesting, and I was seeing him as a man who had many regrets about his selfish past.

One afternoon, he said something about the family that took me in. I don't recall that it was negative, but it opened a door, and I took it. Over the years, he is clearly in denial about the happenings when I was a teen. I asked him to just sit there and listen while I shared what I went through and how it made me feel. As I spoke, he looked like a child to me, sunk into his couch. I could feel some sort of inner freeing. His eyes filled with tears, occasional quiet sobs as he patiently allowed me the time I needed. It doesn't change what happened, but the sorrow and hugs that day did wonders for my heart. Dad died unexpectedly not too long after that.

Ben, Claire, and Mark stayed within a tight circle created with their church community. They all lived in close proximity to each other, and their neighborhood was more of the same. I just never felt good there. In Claire fashion, she would refuse to see myself and Byron, and the others would passively go along with her. Who even knows the things she says and does to create these inclusive bubbles? When she has need for me, she'll be back like nothing ever happened.

Byron, Olivia, and I all live in different states and have little to do with the rest of the family. Although Byron and I remain somewhat close, the bond Olivia has with Claire— being the two who survived the marriage of Mom and Bill together— seems to have affected any relationship she and I may have had. I hope these relationships can find a way to heal. We are so divided. I've tried to locate Jack and Emma, but I heard they moved out of state a long time ago. I haven't found them. I'm sure they wish they had never taken me in.

***

The final day had come. It felt far too soon to be ending already. As we entered the ballroom, the host had collected photos from the past week and was projecting them on the stage for us to see.

I was struck by the contrast from the first day to the last on the friendships that had bonded. How quickly we went from strangers to deeply connected friends. I thought about our lives outside of this conference and imagined they looked similar to mine, where there were few close friends but none that had the time to spend like we had here.

After breakfast, the ushers removed the chairs and tables and helped us gather into a continuous spiral, filling the majority of the ballroom space. All connected into a vortex where the two people at the beginning and end were brought together, closing the chain and asking us to remain hand-in-hand for the final guided meditation.

"Close your eyes if that feels safe, and take a deep, cleansing breath in... and out. Feel the support of the floor beneath you. Know that you are held here, in this space, alongside the others in this room. You are not alone.

Bring your awareness to your breath. Inhale... and exhale... allowing the rhythm to steady you. With each inhale, imagine drawing in energy and support from the people around you, from the earth beneath, and from the universe above.

With each exhale, release tension, fear, or anything that no longer serves you. Now, sense the group as a whole. Feel the presence of others, their hearts and breaths alongside yours. Even without words, you are connected—sharing this moment, sharing this space. Let a quiet gratitude rise for the support you give and receive.

Visualize a soft, warm light forming in your heart. With each breath, allow it to expand outward, connecting to the hearts of everyone here. Feel the warmth, the care, the shared strength. Let this light remind you: you are seen, you are held, you are enough. Take one more deep, grounding breath together—in... and out... slowly. When you're ready, gently open your eyes, carrying this sense of connection, support, and shared presence into the rest of your day."

The silent room then broke out with chatter and laughter. Hugs and movement throughout the room like we were trying to capture a moment we knew was fleeting. People were focusing on their phones and making arrangements to leave.

Numbers and emails were exchanged with the many new friends made, all vowing to stay in touch supporting our journeys. We would meet again next year, but it seemed like forever from this moment. I didn't want to do this alone and really didn't want this to end. Holding back tears of gratitude and sadness for the lonely road ahead. Afraid I would lose this momentum and doubting my ability to go it without them.

Tara looked especially beautiful and happy. She shared that she didn't sleep much but was excited to see her children and husband. She thanked me for our conversation and how an increased love for him was swelling in her heart. She had been planning a wonderful date. They would go into the conversation with a love for each other and the desire to expand and grow together. She expressed how her fears seemed silly now and completely gone after reminiscing on their love story. He texted that he was waiting outside to take her home. We hugged so tight, excited for us all.

I spent some time with our new friends as the room slowly emptied. Gratitude came to me in a very physical way. Filling the center of my heart and expanding with warmth and rays of light, I swear I could see filling the ballroom entirely. I stood in place, making sure to absorb this feeling so I could revisit it whenever I needed. Finally, with my arms holding me tight, I turned to leave and walked past the lines for the shuttle.

My flight wouldn't leave until late tonight, and the hotel provided an extended checkout. I walked around the pond a few times, just absorbing this incredible experience and disbelief that Tara and I were able to reconnect. My mind was bouncing from talks and meditations to new friends and the life I would be returning to. The things I wanted to accomplish to share with them all next year. I decided to finish this lap with a walking meditation of gratitude.

Tears of appreciation, love, and overwhelm flowed. The slight breeze and sunshine felt like hope. I am excited for me and how it felt like my life was changing and for new friends and the ripple effect of our greater understanding. A colorful butterfly passed my view, and I thought of the changes it had to go through to become so beautiful.

When I returned to my room to gather my belongings, I played a video to show the transformation of how the caterpillar had to dissolve most of its body to rebuild itself. We can identify so tightly to this body, but it is just a miraculous vehicle that carries us for part of our journey. Falling all the way apart is part of the journey and what gives us the strength needed to get through this life. Just like the butterfly.

I journaled as fast as I could, writing the lessons and impressions from the retreat so I wouldn't forget. I felt so much love for my friends and our shared journey. I decided I wanted to connect with my family without anchoring us to the past. What could I do that would be an expression of kindness without crossing the protective boundaries established? A small outreach felt like the right place to start. I scheduled a reminder each month to mail Mom a card and to text something light and funny to my siblings—just a small connection, a hopeful bridge.

In gratitude for my body and all that I was learning, I thought of how it had been working so hard to protect me and how I didn't always treat it as a partner in this journey. I wanted to offer better energy and move it, keeping it strong and healthy. I needed to heal the damage I may have caused it to not trust and prioritize daily practice to show appreciation and unity in this new mission.

I wrote a poem and tucked it in my journal as I gathered my things to go. I thought of the stories I have held tight to and worked to dissect them to determine what I needed to let go.

You are not broken—
you are hiding,
curling into the quiet
where the world cannot reach you.

Stop doing that thing that numbs
and distracts
from what aches and waits
in the shadows.

Your body remembers
what your mind longs to forget.

Pain lives in the body,
but so does your courage.

So let it rise,
let it swell,
let it move,
let it release the story you've been carrying.

The life you want
cannot be found in old wounds
or repeated stories,
but in the heart
that refuses to turn away.

Give your body permission
to finally let go.

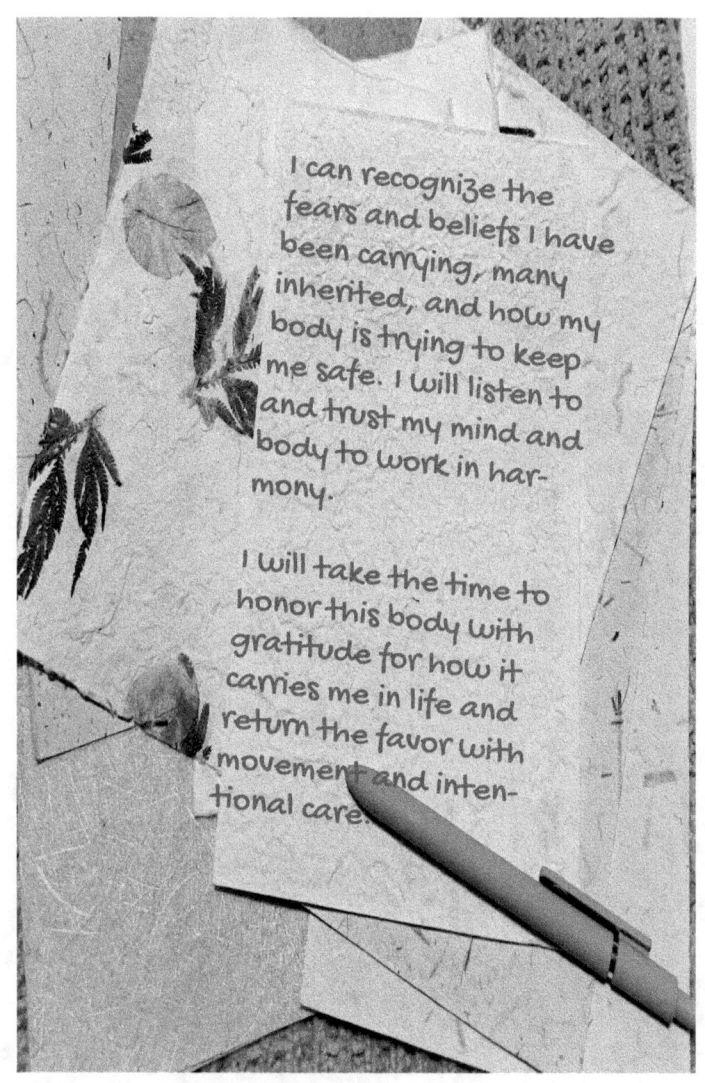

PART FOUR
SPIRIT

"Perhaps our purpose is not found in the answers we seek but in the love we offer and the light we leave behind."

-Cora Ellen Oleson

THIRTY FIVE

"**Welcome back!** What a wonderful series we have had. It is great to see so many familiar faces. Can you feel the energy grow with each new conference? It looks like friendships and meaningful connections have been forged. I'm excited to see the community that has been built. Supporting each other is so important.

We have covered mind and body. Is there anything to us left outside of this physical form? Do we exist outside of this realm? Once our body is no longer viable and we lie down for the last time, are we just fertilizer for what is to come? When our brain waves stop lighting up the monitor, did our lifetime make a difference? Will we be remembered? What contribution did we leave behind? Should we be afraid?

We now reach into the spirit. That thing that gives purpose and meaning. Is this separate from the body and mind? Does our existence end at the edge of what we can see right now? No. I believe that we are infinite beings having a temporary experience. We all will leave what we can see behind. Some will have a long journey and others very short. I believe our spirit is unlimited; the constant which exists beyond this body's life cycle.

We are discovering what is outside of our universe and outside of our mind and body. Evidence that there is so much more; we are just scratching the surface. It is my belief that your desired reality already exists in the quantum field. Open your mind, open your heart. You are a being of infinite potential. When your vibration aligns with what you desire, opportunities begin to manifest.

Intuition, hunches, and ideas that seem to appear out of nowhere. Act on these inspirations. Don't overanalyze or second-guess them. Trust that they are signs of your connection to the universe. Stay focused on your vision while remaining open to how it may come to you. You are opening yourself to miracles.

When the mind, body and spirit move in alignment, life stops feeling like something that happens to us and begins to feel like something we are participating in. To live with this awareness is not to abandon this life, but to inhabit it more fully. To treat each moment as both fleeting and eternal. To listen more carefully. To love more bravely. The same way a wave returns to the ocean without ever having been separate from it.

The universe is flexible - time may not flow in a straight line but fold onto itself, creating loops that constantly intertwine but stay connected. This is a challenging concept to grasp so let me present a show-and-tell to demonstrate. This session will blow your mind!"

He reached for a narrow strip of paper on the table, and held it up between his fingers. "Time, is usually described as a straight line. Or sometimes a circle. But it's neither." As he spoke, he gave one end of the strip a half-twist. "It's this." He taped the ends together. "What had been an ordinary strip is now a loop with a subtle torque in its body, the surface seeming to turn inward on itself." He ran a finger along it, slowly, letting everyone track the movement with their eyes. "A Möbius strip."

He traced the path once. Then again, this time with a marker. "What looks like past and future aren't opposite directions. They're the same surface—folded." His finger crossed the place where the twist lived. "If you move far enough forward, you arrive where you began—but from the other side."

"There is one continuous life, experienced through different orientations of awareness." He turned the strip showing that the inside became the outside without ever crossing an edge. "A past life isn't somewhere else, it's further along the same surface. A future self isn't ahead—it's touching the present.

This may be why moments feel familiar before they happen. You're not remembering something gone. You're brushing against another section of the same surface." He slid a fingertip along the strip again, slower this time."Time travel isn't jumping across distances." He stopped at the twist and gently rotated the loop. "It's changing your orientation. When consciousness passes through the twist, cause and effect can appear to reverse. The future can influence the past. A choice made now can ripple backward. It doesn't change the event—but it changes how it lives in the body."

He cut the strip along the line but it never broke the connection. Laying out the strip to rest open in his palms to show us. He pinched the strip at one point and lifted it slightly. "On a Möbius strip, there is no final ending. When a life completes its circuit, it doesn't disappear. It returns—inverted. As another perspective. Another story. Another self. Different name, same surface." He placed the strip back on the table.

"Are you still with me? Let's talk about collective realities. We are also part of a collective consciousness. Each of our individual signals is interacting with and influencing each other. As you raise your vibration and create a more positive reality for yourself, you are also contributing to the collective elevation of humanity. We can feel that in this room and in our group meditations.

This is a way of being. It's choosing to live each day from a place of limitlessness, connection, and potential. Greater joy, peace, and abundance. You are the architect of your destiny. Stay devoted to your practice and watch as the universe aligns. You are powerful beyond measure. You already have everything you need within you. All the possibilities are in existence simultaneously. Focus on bringing the one you want to you now.

We have focused on the power of our thoughts and work to release what our body stores. What is the meaning in these limited years we experience? Have you ever questioned what comes after this mortal life? Does your answer to this question affect how you live it?

Special guests will be joining us to share their stories throughout this week. You will hear from those who have been near to those leaving this life or experienced crossing over and returned themselves. NDEs or near-death experiences as they are often referred to. Raise your hand if you have heard the term 'near-death experience'. Their stories are inspiring and may make you question long-held beliefs and reassess your goals and aspirations. I ask that you keep your hearts and minds open to what they share and how that feels inside you.

Our team reached out in preparation for this conference and received overwhelming responses. Just to show how common this is, please stand if you have, or know someone who has had experience with something beyond what we can see. Look around and see what I'm seeing. It certainly is more than I thought before taking this journey. Is there something to this? If there is, does that change your life path and the road you wish to travel? You decide. We will devote a large portion of our conference to this topic."

Our host steps aside and holds his hand out to the edge of the stage as a man walks out and trades places with him.

My mind was searching for the information when I initially heard of the Möbius strip. How have I gone this long in life without knowing this concept related to our existence? All I can recall is the relation to inside and outside and magic tricks. Oh! I also remember it coming up in the movie 'Inception'. My mind was blown then too! I looked around to see if anyone else seemed as shook as I was. There were so many things I was hearing and feeling that would take time to process.

***

In a perfectly pressed three-piece suit, a man pulls the microphone off the stand and speaks methodically, appearing to stare to the back of the room over everyone's heads. "Good afternoon, my name is Luke. I have my PhD and work as a research scientist who has published many manuscripts. I am an atheist, or was, and share this with you as my life is focused on provable facts and data. What I experienced went against all I believed in. Now I can see that this is actually not true and have the honor of heading up a team to focus on quantum entanglement and quantum communication. What I will share actually does not go against what I believed but hand in hand with it.

About two years ago, while at my mailbox, I saw a flicker out of the corner of my vision. A neighbor's home was on fire. I ran over yelling to another neighbor who had come outside to call the fire department. I was banging on the door and then started kicking. finally able to get inside. I heard cries from upstairs so taking in a deep breath, I ran to help. She was elderly and had mobility issues and we all tried to help whenever she needed anything. I got to her and made it just out of the room when a blast of fire broke through the attic space above, falling directly on us and pinning my shoulder and arm to the floor. My lungs burned, and things went dark.

When I came to, I knew I was in a hospital and felt someone on my chest. A man was pumping my chest and then pushed so hard - I popped out of my body! I was looking down at the room, watching as they were giving me CPR and was mentally analyzing the situation and surroundings as I was in two places at once. I could sense the panic and chaos in the room but didn't feel any of it myself. No pain either, but I could see my badly burned body below.

My partner from work came into the room, excitedly telling me he had found the answer to the five-year project we had been working on. He motioned for me to follow him, and suddenly we were in the lab where he showed me the breakthrough we had been hoping for. We celebrated, hugging, overwhelmed with relief and joy. I was forming questions in my mind, but before I could finish a thought, the answers were already there. It felt as though information was being poured into me all at once. Not just the answer we were currently working on but all the answers! To everything I ever wondered.

I moved around the familiar lab going from one table to the next, holding up vials of specimen and being able to see down to each cell - without any microscope - just my own vision. I knew the finite details of everything I looked at. Like a child, I was giddy with excitement and was talking at full speed to my partner about this new power I seemed to have.

I paused as my partner was just watching me, amused. He asked if I remembered the fire. Memories flooded my mind in that moment as I looked around the lab a little differently now. His expression shifted, growing somber and told me I had to go back. I didn't want to leave, but he insisted that our work depended on it.

It felt like a vivid dream, but clearer than anything I remember and not choppy like my dreams usually were. This is the only way I can describe what was happening. And just as quickly as I moved into the lab, something pulled me backward the way I had come. I gasped as air rushed into my lungs.

The pain was overwhelming, but when I was able to stay conscious long enough, I asked what happened. I learned that my neighbor inhaled too much smoke and died the following day, that I had some pretty bad burns, and they had lost me briefly but were able to bring me back and that I was going to be okay.

When my wife was allowed in, I was excited to tell her that my partner solved the project. She turned white and told me that she just learned that he had a heart attack and died the Friday before. There was no way he talked to me. It took me time to process that he had died and that him telling me to return now all made a little bit of sense.

The physical recovery was one thing, but grasping what had happened was the battle of a lifetime. The information my partner gave me really did solve the equation and made a remarkable difference in medicine. I searched but could never find evidence that he figured this out before his death. My marriage struggled as I came to understand that the experience with my partner happened in some realm outside of this one. We do exist beyond our body!

I am here to share that there is more. Those who have passed are among us, here to help us. We are not alone. I no longer fear death or believe it is the end of us. This knowledge has changed everything for me. Focusing on what is lasting and what matters most. It has increased my appreciation for life and our body vessel, enhancing my purpose, adjusted my priorities, and improving my relationships. Anything to grow the soul and help others.

Take care of each other and don't lose sight of what is important and lasting. Take care of your brain and body so you will enjoy its abilities to carry you through. Don't be tricked into believing your value lies in the things you accumulate. They are not lasting."

He placed the microphone back in its holster and walked off the stage.

THIRTY SIX

The room fell quiet, as an elderly man practically ran to the front of the stage, quickly introducing himself, being way too close to the microphone. Many of us jumped at the abrupt, loud sound of his voice. "Anston is my name, and boy am I excited to share the good news! For fifteen years, I have worked and volunteered at my local hospice. When I was forced to retire, I just stayed on as a volunteer. They teased that there would only be one way I would leave." He laughed, a laugh that waved across the crowd as we joined him.

"I can't remember what I believed before my time there, but man, the things I saw. I have no doubt that we go on after this life, and no one travels outta here alone! That's my message. I have come here to speak of patients I was with, but also as a son who was with both parents as they crossed over. I can say that the first time I was in the room when this happened, I was totally freaked out, and it took me about a week of not sleeping to get my wits about me.

So in hospice, we know death is at the doorstep. It is a home-like setting, and our care is mainly to keep the patients comfortable, encouraging family to be by their side. We monitor but don't interfere outside of pain management most often. I have been with so many who come out of coma-like states to fully alert and talkative not long before they pass. Sometimes they will talk with me, but most often they look past me and are talking to others I can't see.

I have been told more times than I can count how a loved one is there, someone who is dead but they can see them. They are talking with them and reaching out. Both of my parents have now passed with me in the room. Mom was talking to her long-deceased sister. She told me that her momma was coming to get her tomorrow. She was excited, and just as quickly as she said that, she was asleep but did pass the next day. Just like she said.

Dad never said anything to me, but several days before he passed, you would find him reaching up as if there was something or someone there. I found immense peace and the unwavering knowing that each of us passes from this life with someone we know and are not alone. I'm getting closer to that time myself and look forward to the reunion to come. I believe the hard part is living. Gosh, if you lose your fear of dying, you are less afraid of living!"

As Anston leaves the stage on the right, he is waving at us excitedly. A thirty-something woman walks in from the left. Standing at the microphone so long, I wondered if the microphone was off. Then she spoke with a shaking voice.

"There are a lot of you. My name is Rebecca, and as a very young child, I was abused by my uncle. In my limited vocabulary, I would cry and tell my parents that I didn't want to go with him. He would watch me and my older brother every day in the afternoon until my parents returned from work around dinnertime. As soon as my parents were gone, I stopped crying in hopes he would forget I was there.

My brother went straight to the TV to play video games, leaving me alone with my uncle like always. He used to let me play for a while, but not anymore. He took me upstairs. This time he pushed further than before, and I cried out in pain. He covered my mouth with his hand but didn't stop. His hand was much larger than my face, and it covered my mouth and nose. The pain was more than I could bear and I closed my eyes so tight. I don't think he ever looked at my face, and I didn't have any strength now to try to wriggle out of his grasp.

I felt that I was being lifted. The pain had stopped, and I opened my eyes. I was able to easily take in a breath and found myself in the arms of a dark-haired woman who was softly singing and brushing the hair away from my face. I didn't know who she was, but I wasn't scared. She smiled so warmly and lovingly and told me I was going to be okay. That she was with me and promised she would always be here for me.

I tried to look around to see if my uncle was nearby, but she would tell me to keep her eyes on me and listen to her song. She would rock me until I fell asleep. When I woke up, I was in a strange place with my parents sitting in chairs next to me, holding my hand. I called out for them, and they both jumped up, crying and hugging me.

I didn't understand where I was, but I hurt again, and the woman who had been holding me was gone. The lights were so bright, and I felt cold. Mom covered me with another blanket and climbed on the bed next to me, holding me close. They said I had stopped breathing and was in the hospital now. I was scared to tell them about my uncle, afraid they would be disappointed with me. The abuse continued, but every time, the dark-haired woman came and would hold me and sing to me. My uncle died in a car accident before my next birthday, and I never saw the woman again.

As I got older, I learned that I was in the hospital that day because I died from suffocation. My uncle lied to everyone about how it happened. I believe the dark-haired woman was there to protect me from the abuse, and I worked with a therapist trying to understand why I wasn't saved from it. I have my own feelings on that now but know she removed me from the body that was being abused to comfort me. I only died once, but she visited me every time after.

I can see people's auras clearly everywhere I go. I believe this was a gift I received, and I am working to learn what that means and how I can use it to help others. I firmly believe that we are spiritual beings having an earthly experience. My work is devoted to comforting those who have been hurt like the woman did for me. It's easy for me to find them as they have dim lights. I feel honored to be by their side and help them restore what was taken."

She brushed aside tears that had freely dropped during this time and turned her back to us, walking outside of the bright light and disappearing. A somber cloud sat heavy over us in stark contrast to the excited energy felt earlier. Our host returned to the stage. The silence in the room seemed impossible with the number of people. Not a cough or a breath could be heard.

"A heartfelt thank you to our guests who bravely shared their story. Although I have not had a personal experience, our team has been learning from the work of other organizations devoted to studying this phenomenon. Opening our minds in this way can change what we see, how we act, and what we give meaning to. Compelling data is being gathered showing that many who have died and returned speak of knowing they were co-creators of the lessons their spirit came here to learn and grow from. I know this can be difficult to hear, especially after the stories we have just listened to. They do not say they asked for what was done to them.

Each of us has agency, and within that agency we experience both our own choices and the choices of others. The pain, the joy, and the struggle we live through all matter. We continue to explore this idea—

that each of us comes here to grow and to experience. Many believe that our spirit's learning does not begin and end in a single lifetime, on one plane of existence, or within our limited observable galaxies. Those who have passed beyond their physical bodies often share common descriptions: an existence filled with immense love and peace, a place that feels familiar—like home.

I want to share some of the themes they bring back, because I believe this knowledge can challenge us and help create lasting purpose and meaning in our lives. It has also become my belief that we can experience beyond this physical space even without death. Transcendental meditation and training are taking us further than once believed possible. Teams of researchers are working passionately to understand quantum entanglement more deeply, and we look forward to sharing this work with you in greater depth in the near future. Today, we offer only a glimpse.

We are energized by the learning unfolding in this time and space. I understand that some of this may feel uncomfortable. It challenges long-held beliefs—cultural, religious, and personal—and invites us to loosen what we may be holding tightly.

Because so many answered the call to explore near-death experiences, we have created an opportunity to hear more stories in smaller group settings. We have set up different spaces for you to join. Please be respectful. Our ushers will help you navigate if needed. Thank you for bringing your hearts, for expanding yourselves, and for helping to lift humanity."

There was something powerfully felt with these stories like I had been holding this longing for answers. I could tell that there were many others that were uncomfortable and doubtful. Those of us anxious to get to one of the other rooms to hear more left about a quarter of the ballroom behind. They seemed to recognize the doubts felt and were gathering to share together. Six from our group moved to a smaller room to the right of the ballroom. We got pretty good seats as the room quickly filled, leaving many to stand around the perimeter.

The guest speaker was an older woman sitting at the front of the room facing us with a microphone. There was no raised stage in this room, so I dodged my head around those in front of me to see better but then just closed my eyes to listen to her story. She introduced herself as Annabelle Jane, but everyone knows her as AJ. Her voice sounded shaky, but it didn't seem to be coming from nerves. Just age, I guess. As the room settled in, she began her story.

"I have shared this story numerous times with anyone that wants to hear, although it took me eight years to process it before I had the ability to even put words to what I experienced. Initially, I thought this special gift was just for me until I got the message that I was being selfish and needed to share it. I was flying home from a vacation with my husband when I started to feel a little dizzy and had an atrocious headache.

I covered my eyes and lay down on his shoulder for the remainder of the flight. When we got home, he helped me into the bedroom so I could rest in a dark space.

I tossed and turned trying to get into a position I could sleep, but it felt like my head was splitting open. I cried out, and just then, the room lit up. I opened my eyes, ready to ask why he would turn on the lights, but instead found myself in the most beautiful white space. Not only did I not have a headache, but I had never felt so amazing. I thought I was dreaming, but my senses were sharper than any dream or reality I had experienced.

This space was holding me so tenderly, and I felt a presence behind me. It called me AJ and wrapped me in a hug that was felt throughout. I don't know how else to describe it. When I turned, I could see the face of my Grandpa looking at me with the familiar eyes and smile, but the rest of him was young, no glasses, and he had hair now. I reached up to tousle it as we both laughed.

Memories danced before us. I felt so happy enjoying this time with him and being able to see my young life replayed. I watched myself grow up surrounded by my family and friends. Seeing the wonderful life I was given and feeling immense gratitude for them. We spent so much time together while he took me to moments in time where I could see how my kindness touched others. Choices that made a difference. I also got to see choices I made that hurt people. Some were unintentional, but not all. I had many things I was so ashamed of and embarrassed that he could see them too.

The pain of being there again and seeing the damage I caused brought me pain, both for me and to feel how I made them feel. Wiping tears from my eyes, I looked up at Grandpa, but he was only smiling at me. I didn't feel any judgement, just unconditional love. This view of my life brought me up to the flight and the headache, and I quickly had many questions as I just realized I wasn't in my bed anymore.

Grandpa knew my thoughts before I could share them. He said that I had a blood clot that traveled to my brain and took my life. That I got to return home. We went through what felt like months of questions and answers. He shared that the construct of how we identify: our name, physical description, family, culture, career—is only a temporary house for our spirit who gets to experience many journeys. For my comfort, I got to see him as my grandfather. We have been connected in different ways, but this is the one I am most recently familiar with. These were the messages I received from him.

Understanding must have taken me a while, but I have no concept of the amount of time I spent there. I had the strong feeling wishing I had done more for others and a deep desire to do more. I could see where I played it safe, not standing up for things I believed in outside of my protected world. Only speaking up when it affected me or my immediate family and friends. I avoided politics and stayed in the religion I was born into. I didn't fully believe in the teachings but enjoyed the privileges given me by family and the culture it created. I could see where I wasn't as inclusive as I now wish I had been.

I wish I would have put in the work and effort that could have shown love to others. Even the hard kind. Especially with those outside of the protective bubble I lived in. I believed myself to be Christ-focused, but I never really reached out. I avoided things that were uncomfortable or hard and saw that I was privileged enough to have the option to do so.

Grandpa said it wasn't too late. Although I never wanted to leave this place, I had a deep knowing that my experience would grow my spirit in ways I would miss out on otherwise. And I would be able to come back again. With the desire to do more for others, Grandpa asked, "What will you do differently with this knowledge?" With that, I was traveling across galaxies. Streaks of starlight flew past. I wasn't scared but in wonderment and awe. Back in my bedroom in the dark. My headache was gone, and my clarity sharp. I jumped out of bed to tell my husband what just happened.

I am here with the hope to make you feel comfortable with the message that we get to live this life. Give it your all and don't be afraid to fall or to fail. Any pain or discomfort is temporary. Our days and energy are limited - make the most of what you have. Engage with others and in this life. Who you become in the process is the reward. And don't forget to take care of your mind and body. That will make a difference in the experience and abilities you will have here."

She went on to share some dark days that followed. Depression and sadness accompanied her like never before. She knew it was because she had just left such a loving place, and part of her just wanted to go back. She had to choose to stay and be present in her current role, which was hard. There was soft applause, and many people approached her with hugs of appreciation.

Suffering is often the catalyst to growth. We can grow outside of suffering. Like in Monsters Inc, maybe we can gain far more growth in places of love than suffering can provide. We don't usually do the work when we it is not required.

I created this existence with lessons I chose that would benefit my spirit??!! If this is true, then God isn't rewarding and punishing. We are interacting with others on their journey and we have agency how to act and respond. No matter how awful things seem, we are going to be okay and our experiences will benefit our spirit. So God didn't abandon me! If he rescued me, I wouldn't have had the experiences and growth I need for my spirit!

Maybe we have as many chances as we need to grow, that our destiny is not determined by this experience alone.

THIRTY SEVEN

I'm feeling such a shift in my heart, full of hope. Understanding that I have been waiting for God to bless me and bring me a good life. Thinking that He abandoned me. Wondering if I had any worth or anyone that loved me. Maybe I have this all wrong. The loneliness I have felt and the regrets, believing I have wasted my life and made all the wrong decisions. It is just a journey of experience.

A few more stories I got to hear, speaking to some common messages of love, of guardian angels and helpers, and how they get messages to us. That we got to choose to come here. That we are here to give our spirit experiences that can't be obtained outside of the confusing and hard things we go through, not remembering why we came. How we don't have to die to be more aware of and close to those who can help on this journey. My prayers needed to change from begging and bargaining to gratitude. Now "thank you for the strength to endure, the vision to see, and the heart to listen." The energy and chatter that echoed through the expansive ballroom was palpable. Tara and I were ready to find a new speaker. We walked past the two groups nearest to us, but all the chairs were taken, and we were too far back to hear.

Ushers were scrambling and one told us to follow him, saying this was more popular than they anticipated. He was carrying two chairs and dropped them on the outside of the fourth row for us a few groups away. We had a clear view of the speaker and were able to hear well. A young woman, probably in her very early twenties, was already speaking, so we quietly took our seats. She was looking down at her hands as she spoke. Her voice held excitement.

"I was looking down seeing bodies on the ground near a mangled vehicle. Neither were moving, and there was so much blood. The edges of the surroundings were foggy, and only the accident was in clear focus. I could see skid marks stretched out beyond my view and debris from the vehicle and contents scattered all around them. I could smell gas and the heat of the asphalt, and watched as ambulances arrived. There was so much commotion. It was like I was watching a movie.

I remember observing their panic and looked over the shoulder of the EMT closest to me and saw the face of a girl. I felt great sadness for her and wondered what had happened. They pulled a sheet all the way over her body to include her face, and at that moment, I realized that was me! That was my body!

I didn't feel any connection to it, but I remember her now. Questions and confusion bubbled up when I felt what I can only describe as immense love wrap around me in that thought. I recognized that I felt no pain or even the heavy weight of anxiety that had become my companion for so many years. I only felt all-encompassing love and a welcome stillness. With her entire body covered down there and me here, I realized that I must have died! I watched the ambulance pull away and tried to follow it, but once it got to the edge of the fog, it was gone.

A gentle, levitating pull was drawing me upward. My vision was expanding from where I watched the ambulance moving outward, showing the highway leading to the city, then out further, showing the state, the country, the vast oceans, the entirety of the Earth, through the universe and galaxies. It was so unbelievable the things I got to see and knowledge filled me about everything in depth. I never wanted this to end.

Things went very dark for a moment, and then light fell over me. I found myself surrounded by the most beautiful meadow that went on as far as I could see on every side. I could smell every flower individually and see the details of each petal. There was tall grass, which was a green I had never seen, and it swayed, but there was no wind. The blades moved together, but I could see each one still.

A wisp of a cloud was moving toward me, and the form of a woman appeared out of it, but she wasn't clear like this meadow. She smiled at me, and I felt her thoughts! I heard and felt love, calmness, and the most penetrating knowing that I was precious and known. Overcome with the message that my soul yearned for. The understanding that my body did die, and I am home again. She let me know that she was my guide and had been with me on this earthly journey.

We sat together in this meadow, and I got to see wonderful memories from my life. As we progressed, I also got to see great sadness. I felt the hard things all over again like I was back in those moments, and it tore my heart to see how I hurt myself and others and how others hurt me. I didn't want to see anymore and asked her to make it stop. She did.

She impressed on me what a privilege it is to experience life in a body. How the emotions and forgetting where we came from are also part of that physical existence. I then had a remembering of how I yearned for this experience and helped create the plan for the growth I wanted to gain! This really hit me hard as I had believed that God gave me trials and I was here to endure them. If I did what he wanted and prayed enough, He would bless me. A game to win. This was wrong - where did I get that idea?

I also saw that I hadn't finished what I set out to do, and these things couldn't be found in this lovely place but required a body to complete. My guide told me everything would be okay anyway, but I pushed a little that I didn't want to leave it like that; I had so much I wanted to do. I asked if I could go back for a little longer.

Sweetly, I felt her answer that my body was badly damaged and I was to stay here. She seemed fine with that but I didn't feel the same. Why I would plan a purpose for my journey and leave before it was completed? She was patient with me and when I was done, she shared that our paths are not set and our agency allows us to choose different outcomes based on our actions and others' actions. That these different paths all exist within us in possibility and each one provides growth.

The incredible beauty and warm love I felt around me was at war with my longing for the body that was trying but failed to fulfill her chosen mission. I remember the pain and heartache there and even felt the question in myself on why I would want to return and leave this glorious place. Especially if I didn't have to. One of the deepest memories that I got to see from my life was that I didn't feel that I mattered, didn't feel loved, and longed for a place I belonged. But here, I knew I was loved and I knew I was home. On Earth, those feelings existed only in the forgetting from where I came and where I would return and that the emotions are stuck in the body. I wondered then if the body is the veil spoken of.

Information was being downloaded into my heart and mind so rapidly. I remembered that the growth I needed could be found there in the hard things and not in this beautiful place. That I needed a body to make it happen, especially if I wanted to become a mother. What I did next could be described as a toddler's tantrum. Trying to convince her to give me what I wanted. We talked for a while as she shared that if I did return, I would need to be especially strong for my children to help them on their journeys. She let me see what she meant.

Now I knew that I had to return! I asked to replay the accident again and again and came up with a plan to return and how it could work. I could change how the accident happened just enough to let my body survive. My guide shared that more time may not equal the outcome I hoped for. To help me understand, I was shown a future of many struggles where ultimately, she pulled away from everything and everyone that could hurt her.

Without the memory of this moment, I may find that going back to save her from this accident wouldn't have helped her fully live. I then asked if I could also return one more time later in her journey to give the message of hope that the earthly experience was just a tiny moment, a gift that she wanted, and that she is deeply loved and to keep going?

Here it was easy to understand that folding dimensions was possible so I knew I could help myself. Could I try? My guide was present in my thoughts. Her smile told me that this is my choice. She said she would be given the gift of self-healing, which would be needed in times to come. I practiced the plan since I knew of the fear and panic the body holds could make me forget what I came to do. I hugged my guide so tightly as she pointed down to the road that led to the accident, and I could see the vehicle coming into view. It was time!

I felt like I was a fully bloomed flower trying to squeeze back into the seed. Losing all the beauty of the meadow and traveling quickly through the void. Oh, it was painful, but I knew I had to keep going. There I was seeing the road racing in front of me. Panic and fear were felt through every cell as I focused straight ahead on the task. I was ejected, and horrendous pain overcame me. I felt myself lift away from my body again and above the accident. As soon as I left the body, the pain was completely gone.

My guide was there waiting for me. We watched as the EMT kneeled at my body's side, and I again peered over his shoulder to see her... my face. This time there was an oxygen mask on her...me. I could sense that I was both on that stretcher and here watching and was in awe of the limitlessness of the creation.

I threw my arms around my guide and squealed with joy, "IT WORKED!!" Elation and so much energy danced around us in sparkling swirls, celebrating. As the ambulance disappeared into the fog, we were back again in the beautiful meadow. We got right to work, where I received instructions for my next return. Reminded that I am to share my story of the accident, crossing over, and not interfere further. I was told that simply sharing my story would get the message where it needed to be.

My guide would send me when it was time, so I practiced over and over while loving and exploring the meadow around me. I had to practice because when I didn't, the memory of her and that life was slipping away.

It was time. I waved goodbye and watched as the meadow got further from me. Coldness and emptiness overtook everything. I became scared as the memory of my mission was fading. I kept repeating out loud that I just needed to share my story. By the time I made it through the tiniest opening, I didn't know where I was or why I was there. I heard a voice that said, "Share your story." When I looked back, there was nothing but a busy road.

Surrounded by concrete and buildings, I wandered around for hours looking for anything or anyone that looked familiar. I was lost. I stopped as I was now at a corner where people were crossing in many directions and wondered which way I should go. I turned away from the street and looked up at the large building trying to adjust to the heaviness I felt and the confusion as to where I was. A woman who appeared agitated looked over and started walking quickly toward me.

She said she had been waiting for me, and I was late. She seemed to know who I was, so I followed her quick steps and asked what I was late for. She slowed down briefly, looking strangely at me, and said I was a guest speaker for their conference. I was about to stop but then felt a little shove from somewhere behind me and knew to follow her. I remembered that I was to share this story.

I am here to do just that. I need to tell you that I died in that initial accident—but that was not the end. I returned home. It was familiar, filled with a warmth of unconditional love unlike anything felt here. I was no longer identified with a body, or even the name she once carried. The message I want to share is that as beautiful as the meadow is, don't rush to arrive there sooner. You will long for the experience that only this place—this life—can offer. If you have loved ones who did rush, know that they are all welcomed home as you will be. Never too soon or too late.

We have guides who help us along the way in a life we were part of creating. Don't despair. You are here to experience much. You chose to come, and you helped choose the lessons you wished to learn. Try not to feel lonely—you are connected to everything! You are more than your body. Care for it, but don't let it become your identity or distract you from your purpose. Love is what you came from, and love is what you are meant to carry into this world. Your life here matters in ways you cannot measure.

Kindness matters. Every small act. Care for every living thing. Express compassion. Even in suffering—especially in suffering—become the person you would be proud to have been. Live fully. Build beautiful relationships. Some may last no longer than a warm smile, but they matter. This is only a moment, and you have things to do. Nothing meaningful is ever lost. Find joy in the journey. Don't forget to have some fun. Whatever you do, don't give up. You will all be home before you know it."

She smiled warmly looking over the crowd that had gathered. "I went from being dead at the scene to only having this...." she reached down. Tara grabbed my arm and was pointing at her mole and then at the speaker. She had the same mole in the same place we did! As she pulled up the leg of her pant, I saw my scar.

About the Author

Cora Ellen Oleson's work is drawn from her life experiences and presented as semi-autobiographical fiction. The conference and the quantum entanglement with other versions of herself were created as a fictional resolution. Names and identifying details have been changed to protect those she loves and all who have taken part in her journey.

TikTok
tiktok.com/@cora.ellen.oleson

YouTube
youtube.com/@CoraEllenOleson

Instagram
instagram.com/cora.ellen.oleson/

www.ingramcontent.com/pod-product-compliance
Lightning Source LLC
LaVergne TN
LVHW021759060526
838201LV00058B/3154